REASONS TO REASON IN PRIMARY MATHS AND SCIENCE

REASONS TO REASON IN PRIMARY MATHS AND SCIENCE

ALISON BORTHWICK
ALAN CROSS

$SAGE

Los Angeles | London | New Delhi
Singapore | Washington DC | Melbourne

Learning Matters
An imprint of SAGE Publications Ltd
1 Oliver's Yard
55 City Road
London EC1Y 1SP

SAGE Publications Inc.
2455 Teller Road
Thousand Oaks, California 91320

SAGE Publications India Pvt Ltd
B 1/I 1 Mohan Cooperative Industrial Area
Mathura Road
New Delhi 110 044

SAGE Publications Asia-Pacific Pte Ltd
3 Church Street
#10-04 Samsung Hub
Singapore 049483

Editor: Amy Thornton
Production Controller: Chris Marke
Project Management: Swales & Willis Ltd, Exeter,
Devon
Marketing Manager: Lorna Patkai
Cover design: Wendy Scott
Typeset by: C&M Digitals (P) Ltd, Chennai, India
Printed in the UK

Library of Congress Control Number: 2018939032

British Library Cataloguing in Publication Data

A catalogue record for this book is available from
the British Library

ISBN 978-1-5264-3503-3
ISBN 978-1-5264-3504-0 (pbk)

At SAGE we take sustainability seriously. Most of our products are printed in the UK using responsibly sourced papers
and boards. When we print overseas we ensure sustainable papers are used as measured by the PREPS grading
system. We undertake an annual audit to monitor our sustainability.

CONTENTS

ACKNOWLEDGEMENTS

This book is the product of much thinking and reasoning about mathematics and science. It draws on the ideas that we developed in our first two books on the connections between mathematics and science and the place of curiosity across the primary STEM subjects.

Since then we have continued to consider these connections, helped along the way by a large number of people whose work, conversations and comments have contributed and shaped our thinking further. These contributions have been drawn from individual conversations with teachers and learners, larger group discussions at various conferences, both in the UK and internationally, and colleagues and friends who have supported and challenged us.

Many of these people may not even realise the role of their contributions and we are only sorry we cannot thank them all personally. However, a number of people have played a visible part in making this book possible and we would like to acknowledge them here.

Bluegate Field Primary School, Tower Hamlets

Broadoak Primary, Salford

Chapel Break Infant School, Norwich

Horning Primary School, Norfolk

Lodge Lane Infant School, Norwich

Malmsbury Primary School, Tower Hamlets

Mauldeth Road Primary School, Manchester

Moss Park Junior School, Trafford

Seven Mills Primary School, Tower Hamlets

St. Pauls CE (Crompton Street), Salford

St. Peters CE Primary, Tameside

West Winch Primary School, Norfolk

Cherri Moseley, freelance mathematics consultant and author

Colleagues at NRICH, University of Cambridge

Adrian Bowden, Travelling Science

Jon Board, freelance science consultant and author

ABOUT THE AUTHORS

Alison Borthwick

Alison has a wealth of UK and international experience in mathematics education. She is the strategic mathematics adviser for The Evolution Academy Trust and a part-time freelance education and mathematics consultant. She continues to work with the University of Cambridge, the University of Manchester, the Royal Society and other educational establishments across the UK and abroad. She is an active member of BSRLM, NAMA and is the current chair of the joint Primary MA/ATM association. Follow Alison on Twitter @easternmaths or find her on LinkedIn.

Alan Cross

Alan teaches primary science, DT and computing at the University of Manchester, as well as providing CPD in primary science and DT and writing about science for primary students and teachers. As well as acting as a school governor, Alan works as an external examiner and has contributed to primary science projects around the world. Recent publications include: *Essential Primary Science* (2009, OUP/McGraw Hill) and *Creative Ways to Teach Primary Science* (2014, OUP/McGraw Hill). Alan tweets about primary STEM subjects at @AlanBryceCross

Alison and Alan are also the co-authors of the recently published books on *Connecting Primary Maths and Science* (2016, OUP/McGraw Hill) and *Curious Learners in Primary Maths, Science, Computing and DT* (2016, Sage). They have both written numerous articles for UK and international journals.

ABOUT THIS BOOK

Much is said in educational circles – both nationally and internationally – about the importance of learners being enabled to reason. In the information age our need to remember and recall huge quantities of knowledge may be diminishing. At the same time the importance of understanding may be growing. Human civilisation, nations and communities need individuals who seek and achieve understanding so that problems can be solved, and solutions found. To be successful citizens we will need to reason about the world, we might see **reasoning as the currency of the future**! For primary teachers at present there are calls to promote reasoning but little in terms of concrete advice to make this real in classrooms and schools. Our interest in the primary science, technology, engineering, mathematics (STEM) subjects of mathematics and science has led us naturally to consider reasoning in primary classrooms. One prerequisite is that teachers themselves seek a greater understanding of reasoning, hence our title *Reasons to Reason*. This book offers a framework of ideas, models, skills and practical ideas which teachers can use with immediate effect in both mathematics and science lessons. Before embarking on this journey we consulted with different groups of teachers and student teachers, through focus groups and questionnaires, on their understanding of reasoning. While these were small samples, the data consistently revealed a need to support primary teachers with this subject. We have written this book with those teachers in mind and believe it offers all teachers a toolkit for reasoning.

Organisation and structure of the book

This is a book that can be dipped into or read from cover to cover. Its purpose is to encourage the development of learners' reasoning skills.

All of the chapters have elements that permeate through them. For example, we have included Reasoning Focus and Reflection boxes that encourage you to stop, think and reason. Try This! boxes are offered for you to try some of the ideas in classrooms and across the school, with a variety of stakeholders. At the beginning and end of each chapter you will find a summary of bullet points that allow you to have a snapshot of the contents. Chapters 4 to 7 focus particularly on the **skills of reasoning**. In these chapters you will find a wealth of activities linked to the skills of reasoning, to use across the primary age range in mathematics and science classrooms. This book is designed to equip you with the knowledge, the ideas and the skills to enable learners to reason in primary mathematics and science. In short it gives you the reasons to reason!

Chapter 1 is designed to support the understanding and development of reasoning for teachers. It explores the place of reasoning in mathematics and science, and considers different definitions, reflecting on the link between thinking and reasoning, as well as including some evidence from teachers about their views of reasoning and what it looks like in the classroom. Whatever your current perception and knowledge of reasoning, we hope this chapter prompts you to consider to what extent we include reasoning explicitly in the classroom.

Chapter 2 explores different frameworks which teachers could use to support the teaching of reasoning within their classrooms. It offers a list of the **skills of reasoning** that we have collected together and considers how we might use them in mathematics and science lessons.

Chapter 3 focuses on the Early Years and considers the place and purpose of thinking and reasoning. It recognises that young children can reason but that the practitioner will have an important role to play in developing thought. The chapter points out that all young children reason, but that this might not be easily recognisable if adults expect learners to be little adults.

Chapter 4 looks at the skill of questioning within reasoning. It considers the different types of questions that could usefully be asked to encourage learners to draw on different skills of reasoning. It also suggests that learners should be encouraged to ask more questions.

Chapter 5 considers the many ways in which learners' predictions contribute to science and mathematics, and how these allow learners to think in a more abstract way about the future. Prediction can occur at any primary age as learners can speculate about the relationship between events and values. Informed prediction means we can have a degree of confidence about what will occur.

Chapter 6 explores how pattern spotting and using data are great springboards for reasoning opportunities. This is not about mindless pattern spotting but rather a focus on mindful learning, which Langer (1997) describes as an awareness of the conditionality of knowledge. Treating knowledge as 'conditional', in that it holds certain conditions, can help to raise awareness and allow learners to begin to reason, rather than simply taking knowledge as unquestioned givens. Using data is a great example, as we all know that while graphs and charts hold to certain conditions, the interpretation of the data – depending on how it has been presented, for example – is often open to many possibilities.

Chapter 7 positions reasoning within problem-solving and investigation. While reasoning has many skills that we associate with it, problem-solving and investigation have a different set of strategies. We might be trying to solve a problem by finding all the possibilities. Reasoning supports this by drawing on particular **skills of reasoning**, such as pattern spotting or questioning.

Chapter 8 asks, 'How do we evidence reasoning?' It explores a variety of opportunities that we can use to potentially capture how learners reason, both practically and also by suggesting that if learners are justifying, generalising and seeking proof, they are using some of the most important hallmarks of being a mathematician or scientist, whatever their age!

Chapter 9 concludes the book by considering what a culture of reasoning could look like across a school. Throughout the first eight chapters, we include development opportunities. These are suggestions which teachers, subject/senior leaders, other adults, parents, governors and learners could try out in a variety of situations to begin to promote and recognise reasoning. This final chapter gathers all of these suggestions together so that schools can start to develop their own toolkit in order to cultivate a culture of reasoning.

Why does this book focus on two subjects: mathematics and science?

We have argued strongly (Cross and Borthwick, 2016) that while they are distinct subjects, mathematics and science overlap educationally in many ways. Subject boundaries, while widely recognised, are artificial; primary teachers will be aware that many primary-aged learners do not readily acknowledge these boundaries. Both school subjects require reasoning in order to solve problems, investigate and more. We feel that primary teachers teaching both subjects are in a great position to get the very best out of these STEM subject links.

REFLECTION

Is reasoning most often associated with a particular subject? For some would that be mathematics?

This is also an exciting and important time in education, as countries, including the UK, begin to recognise the need for learners to be competent in both mathematics and science skills as we move into the next technological revolution. Does this explain at least part of the enormous interest in the international TIMSS (Martin et al., 2016) and PISA (OECD, 2017) comparison reports? Now more than ever, learners around the world need to be competent in the skills associated with a STEM curriculum.

More recently teachers and educators have begun to talk about science capital. A person's science capital is all the science-related knowledge, understanding, attitudes, experiences and social contacts that she or he has (Godec et al., 2017). This is the sum of your knowledge of science, how to teach it, your interest in science, the science you have done, science-related movies, people you encounter who know/do/value science. This is your science capital.

This idea is based on the writing of Pierre Bourdieu (1930–2002) who was concerned with the way a person's 'capital' affects their life chances. Godec et al. (2017) promote a classroom approach which seeks to make explicit and build on an individual's science capital.

In a similar way do you possess mathematics capital, STEM capital? Even reasoning capital? Much of this book advocates in teachers and learners an engagement with one's own understanding and experience, one's personal reasoning about the world of science and mathematics. Thus, another angle on metacognition.

1
A RATIONALE FOR REASONING

IN THIS CHAPTER

By the end of this chapter you will:

- have considered definitions of thinking and reasoning;
- understand how thinking and reasoning are similar yet different;
- be able to begin to identify **skills of reasoning**;
- have reflected upon the place of reasoning in at least two primary STEM subjects.

Introduction

This chapter will introduce you to a number of important ideas around how primary-aged learners can, do and could reason within their mathematics and science education. As well as explanations and illustrations the chapter will give examples and opportunities to reflect and reason yourself.

The ability to question, pose, investigate and solve problems is at the heart of mathematics and science. However, until a problem has first been understood, learners may struggle to engage with it. This presents learners with many difficulties, because there is a great deal involved in solving a problem; a fact that is often unappreciated. There are many skills involved in unravelling what a problem is about, which concepts and skills are needed and how to make use of them in finding a possible solution. Some of the required knowledge and skills will be subject-specific, some will be common to mathematics and science – for example, measurement.

Even when learners are equipped with several different investigative and problem-solving strategies they still need toreason which one to use. Reasoning is essential to children learning more and solving problems. It is the one element that binds together all the different skills needed to solve a problem (skills such as pattern spotting, offering conjectures, generalising). Without reasoning, learners may be simply following procedures, applying rules, ignoring patterns and missing opportunities. While this book is about reasoning, we acknowledge that this is one of several strands that learners need to draw on to be mathematically or scientifically proficient. Kilpatrick et al. (2001) offer five different strands: conceptual understanding, procedural fluency, strategic competence, productive disposition and adaptive reasoning (see Chapter 7). They view these strands as equally important and interdependent. Being able to draw on each of these stands when solving problems and carrying out investigations is key to being successful in these two STEM subjects – and without the reasoning strand, learners may struggle to make progress, connect ideas and knowledge and reach a level of understanding that is not simply about producing a formula or memorising a fact. So, what is reasoning?

What is reasoning?

The word 'thinking' is used in everyday language and we use it in different ways. For example, *Anne is sure to think of a solution* (an action); *What do you think about the decision to cut down these trees to enable a housing developing?* (seeking an opinion); *Why didn't you think of that before you went ahead with that idea?* (a kind of foresight).

Types of thinking have been described by different people. We do not have space here to examine these in detail but Frank Williams' (1969) taxonomy lists eight types of creative thinking:

fluency: the capacity to generate ideas, possible responses to a problem or situation

flexibility: coming up with alternatives, different ideas

originality: generation of new unique solutions

elaboration: the development or expansion of ideas to make them more comprehensible/interesting

risk-taking: experimenting, trialling, challenging ideas

complexity: applying logic, establishing order, identify missing parts

curiosity: wondering, puzzling

imagination: the ability to see a mental picture, new ideas, new possibilities

It is interesting to note that reasoning is not explicitly mentioned in Williams' list.

In talking with teachers and reflecting about thinking and reasoning, we have settled on a definition that, for us, is a point of reference which we can draw on when exploring reasoning in primary classrooms:

> *Reasoning is thinking,*
>
> *but it is thinking in a logical, purposeful, goal-directed way.*

We have selected the words carefully within our definition. To apply some logic assumes that alternative viewpoints have been considered; to have purpose implies that we are focused and determined in pursuing our line of enquiry; and to have a goal suggests that there is an objective in mind, but this does have to be a final answer or a proof – this could be the process we have been engaged with or the knowledge we have gained along the way. We purposefully did not include the word 'correct' in our definition. This is because, for us, reasoning is how we navigate through a problem, to try and make sense of the situation, to select the tools to help us and to reach some sort of resolution, even if this is to continue to reason! We also believe that all learners can reason, despite researchers such as Inhelder and Piaget (1958) suggesting that learners' ability to reason is quite limited until around the age of 12 years old.

So, for us, reasoning is another type of thinking, some may even say a subset of thinking. In some cases it is about finding reasons for things, making decisions, considering cause and effect, wondering, What is the reason for this happening? While reasoning is not mentioned in Williams' (1969) list of thinking, it would contribute to all his types of thinking if we applied our definition to it.

How do reasoning and thinking fit together?

Thinking is that exercise of the mind which forms ideas, conceptions, conditions, recognitions, revisions, considerations, connections, opinions, judgements, imaginings and intentions. Since our brains are so very active it is perhaps no surprise that we have so many terms associated with thinking. Reasoning is a form of thinking; words such as logical and systematic often preface. But thinking can be disordered, illogical and messy. Reasoning is, according to Fowler and Fowler (1984), *the action of thinking in a logical, sensible way even if the outcome if incorrect*. Reasoning brings with it a certain order (often subjective and pertinent to that person); it suggests clarity and logic.

REFLECTION

When do you reason in your day-to-day life? When making a purchase? Choosing what to eat? Which route to take to work?

The terms 'reasoning' and 'thinking' are often used interchangeably. On one level this is understandable and acceptable, but on another, it de-values the importance of reasoning and the skills associated with it.

To assist your understanding, take a moment to look at the options below. For each, consider does this require thought? Does it require the logical, purposeful, goal-orientated thought we call reasoning?

Do these situations require reasoning?

(a) Choosing a birthday present for a friend.

(b) Deciding how to vote in a referendum.

(c)   Selecting a new pair of shoes.

(d)   Deciding how to pay for the purchase of a house.

Each scenario requires thought. Options a) and c) might, in some circumstances, require little thought or in others more than that. Options b) and d), it might be argued, require more thought and the weighing of options and consideration of rationale we associate with reasoning. Equally, different people will employ different **skills of reasoning** for each scenario. For some, buying a pair of shoes is a fairly straightforward experience which may require some reasoning, but for others it may require many more reasoning skills.

By now you are probably thinking I need one definition for thinking and one for reasoning. You are reasoning about reasoning!

What do others say about thinking and reasoning?

There are many varied and interesting definitions of thinking and reasoning.

> *Thinking is using thought or rational judgment while reasoning is to persuade, or move by argument, to express in logical form.*

> (Fowler and Fowler, 1984)

> *Mathematical thinking is more than being able to do arithmetic or solve algebra problems. In fact, it is possible to think like a mathematician and do fairly poorly when it comes to balancing your checkbook. Mathematical thinking is a whole way of looking at things, of stripping them down to their numerical, structural, or logical essentials, and of analyzing the underlying patterns. Moreover, it involves adopting the identity of a mathematical thinker.*

> (Devlin, 1991)

> *Probably the single most important lesson is that being stuck is an honorable state and an essential part of improving thinking.*

> (Mason et al., 2010)

> *Reasoning is fundamental to knowing and doing mathematics. Reasoning enables children to make use of all their other mathematical skills and so reasoning could be thought of as the 'glue' which helps mathematics make sense.*

> (Pennant et al., 2014)

> *Adaptive reasoning refers to the capacity to think logically about the relationships among concepts and situations. Such reasoning is correct and valid, stems from careful consideration of alternatives, and includes knowledge of how to justify the conclusions.*

> (Kilpatrick et al., 2001)

In considering the different definitions of thinking and reasoning we asked teachers what their views were. We have included one example to show how we collected these definitions, and a summary (Figure 1.1).

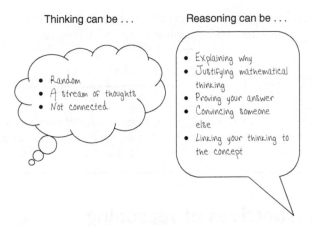

Thinking can be . . .

- Random
- A stream of thoughts
- Not connected

Reasoning can be . . .

- Explaining why
- Justifying mathematical thinking
- Proving your answer
- Convincing someone else
- Linking your thinking to the concept

Figure 1.1 An example of the differences between thinking and reasoning given by a group of teachers

Table 1.1 Definitions of thinking and reasoning

What is thinking?	What is reasoning?
Thinking can be recalling facts.	Reasoning is a form of thinking.
Thinking can be exploring, pondering.	Reasoning is purposeful, a logical progression.
Thinking can be open-ended, abstract, no particular end point.	Reasoning is trying to make sense of things; it is deeper than thinking.
Thinking can be everyday thoughts, uncoordinated.	Reasoning is about logic, deeper thinking, convincing, proving, explaining.
Thinking can be a cognitive process that doesn't always culminate in a product.	Reasoning is the why and the how.
Thinking can be low level recognition or consideration of ideas.	Reasoning often uses more than one idea or concept to amend, develop or establish concept.

The teachers we consulted all perceived reasoning to be a higher order skill than thinking. They believed that reasoning required thinking but you could think without reasoning.

REFLECTION

What do you think? Is reasoning a higher order skill than thinking?

However, many of the teachers also commented that they had not really considered the difference before we asked them to, and confessed they were probably using the words inter-changeably. While this is not a problem within everyday language and conversation, within an educational context there is a difference, because, as we show in Chapter 2, reasoning has many important and necessary skills which mathematics and science draw heavily on, that are different to reasoning, in that they are logical, purposeful and goal-directed.

┌─────────────────── **TRY THIS!** ───────────────────┐

Have a ten-minute discussion with colleagues to consider the difference between thinking and reasoning. Collate their responses on a flip chart and display it in the staff room for a few weeks/ half a term. Invite teachers and teaching staff to reflect on and add to the list.

└──┘

Historical perspectives of reasoning

Reasoning has a history, perhaps going right back to the time when our ancestors became aware of themselves and developed an ability to think. Did they reason that life in a dry cave was more comfortable than outside? Did they reason that piles of stones could be arranged with wooden timbers to make a human-made cave? A shelter, a dry, potentially warm and safe place to live?

Ancient Greece is seen as the birthplace of modern thoughtful endeavour including philosophy, mathematics, logic and scientific method. Socrates (470–399 BC) was famous for a form of discussion or argumentation about ideas, the Socratic method. Plato (428–348 BC) wrote of the value of abstract ideas. He saw them as more powerful than observation of reality. Their contemporary, Aristotle (384–322 BC), formed the basis of much Western philosophy and he had a profound effect on science following his study of and writing about topics including optics, motion and biology. These and other thinkers (Abu Nasr Al-Farabi, 872–950 AD) showed that rational thought could take humans forward. Such thinking could seek explanation and extrapolate from one observation or idea to another. Many early ideas were later proved wrong, but crucially they were thoughts, they were rational and they empowered others ultimately to challenge these ideas and seek better alternatives.

Why do we need reasoning?

Why do people need to reason?

Humans may be the only sentient organisms which reason. Our ability to reason allows us to develop ideas and artefacts which benefit ourselves and the world. Could reasoning be the currency of the future? We use reasoning in games, in our work, in pastimes and in relationships. In fact, games like chess are often promoted as opportunities to develop reasoning. To gain an understanding of learners' reasoning we often use theoretical models (e.g., Piaget, Vygotsky, Bruner). These theories are themselves sets of ideas where we and others reason about their potential.

Why do we need reasoning in mathematics and science?

Mathematicians and scientists need to reason. They need to observe and recognise features and explanations relating to values, relationships, patterns and phenomena. Science includes facts to be learned. Mathematics is a subject based on rules that need to be explored. Without reasoning, much of mathematics and science would be under-developed and perhaps would remain unknown to us – for example, Galileo's reasoning that the four objects he observed early in 1610 moving close to Jupiter were not stars but Jupiter's moons and that Jupiter and its moons were a model of our solar system (a sun orbited by planets and moons) (White, 2007).

Why do we need reasoning in mathematics and science education?

Both of these subjects run the risk of being taught in an abstract, procedural way. Reasoning can prevent this by encouraging learners to notice, reflect, question and explore. If we do not include reasoning within mathematics and science curricula we are not enabling learners for the future.

Many mathematics educators (e.g., Pennant et al., 2014; Nunes et al., 2009) have considered reasoning to be one of the essential components in mathematics education. However, reasoning often lacks the attention in the curriculum that mathematical content knowledge is given (e.g., learners' ability to recall number facts). Subject knowledge content is essential to children learning mathematics. But if we do not teach this content alongside reasoning, opportunities to extend learning are missed. Look at the following mathematics example. The calculation could be completed with very little reasoning, but what does the reasoning component add to the questions that follow it?

REASONING FOCUS

Solve this calculation: $14 \times 5 = ?$

Have you reached an answer?

How did you work it out?

Which method or strategy did you use?

Can you solve it a different way? And another? And another?

Reason: Which method is the quickest? Easiest? Most efficient?

Look in the Appendix for some possible solutions.

Science can also be abstract but primary science is usually focused on everyday phenomena which can often, but not always, be observed directly; for example, the insulation of sound, the appearance of shadows, the growth of a seedling. Reasoning assists young scientists with things that puzzle them, such as explanations, links, questioning, problem-solving. Reasoning supports the learner who looks at a situation or a phenomenon such as a rainbow and applies thought. They might utilise (see Chapter 2) one or more of the six powerful words: Why? When? How? Where? Who? What? For example, Why does a rainbow form? When does a rainbow form? How does a rainbow form? Where does a rainbow form? Who might contribute to answers or investigations? What causes a rainbow to form?

Primary mathematics and science are often concerned with questions, predictions, data and patterns. Looking at the graph in Figure 1.2, can we extrapolate from the data presented to suggest a figure for the world population in 2051? Could we reason and consider factors which might influence how steep the line will be? Food supply? Health? Birth rate?

Cross and Borthwick (2016) quote Haylock (2010) and The Royal Society (2014) when they argue strongly for links between primary school mathematics and science. Connecting mathematics with science makes sense because the skills strongly overlap between the two STEM subjects. Often when we talk about mathematics and science we reference the specific subject knowledge content (such as fractions in mathematics or plants in science). However, we need to remember that while both subjects have prescribed content knowledge, the **skills of reasoning** are applicable to both.

We have already suggested that questioning is imperative to reasoning in mathematics and science education. Consider these six sentence stems and how they engender a reasoning atmosphere: Why?, When?, How?, Where?, Who?, What?

Mathematics example – Does the multiplication of two or more numbers always result in a larger number?

Why? Why do you think multiplication results in a larger product?

When? When you multiply numbers together, what is happening mathematically?

How? How could we multiply numbers together?

Where? Where can I find an example that offers a counter example?

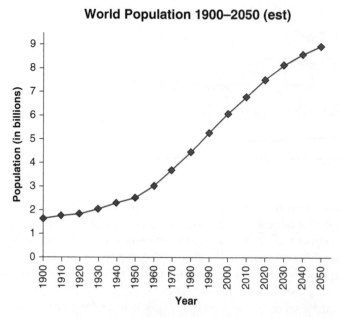

Figure 1.2 Estimated growth in the world population of humans on Earth

Who? Who could prove or disprove this question?

What? What do I need to do first?

Science example – Can sound travel around corners?

Why? Why does it travel like this?

When? When can sound travel?

How? How do we know how sound travels?

Where? Where does sound travel?

Who? Who can tell us more?

What? What do I need to do to find out more?

Without reasoning in mathematics and science education, learning would be very limited.

─── **TRY THIS!** ───

Go on a reasoning walk around the school. What evidence can you spot of learners' and adults' reasoning?

How do we reason?

There are a number of stages that learners might go through when they are reasoning. These are related to the skills we explore in Chapter 2 which looks at **skills of reasoning**. *How* we reason is a process we go through; often with stages intertwined with each other and not always in the order below. Look at the suggestions below.

- noticing;
- talking and listening;
- making sense;
- sharing insights;
- metacognition.

The importance of noticing

If we do not notice something, how can we begin to reason about it? To notice something means we have made some observations – perhaps we have been surprised or ambushed in some way, but it has caused us to question, stop, pause, reflect, think and then we begin to reason. We believe noticing is particularly important in reasoning.

The importance of talking, listening, sense-making and sharing insights

Talking and listening are particularly important for learner reasoning. Primary teachers will generally agree that learner talk and discussion in lessons is very important. We want to emphasise here how very important talk is in the development of reasoning in both science and mathematics.

Reasoning is about thinking and making sense of the world. Sense-making is something that individuals do as they assimilate ideas and accommodate (Piaget, 1970) new ideas in relation to those previously held. Vygotsky (1978) talked of each learner's internal world of thought 'inner speech' which then develops through our making thoughts external (e.g., sharing them).

One way we do this is through Barnes' (1992) 'exploratory talk' in social settings, in this case, classrooms. The zone of proximal development (Vygotsky, 1978) describes the area where a child learns in the presence of a knowing other, adult or child. Communication, much of it verbal, will be through talk. Therefore Mercer's (2008) objective of 'fluent and reflective speakers' is not only the objective of education but also the means to learn, developing through its expression.

This has an advantage for teachers because in order for us to assess understanding prior to teaching we need to perceive children's thought. Our only way of doing this is through verbal interaction alongside observation of behaviour and of children's written work. Learners need to interact, to share insights, but much more important than that for reasoning is the idea of 'inter-thinking' – that is, thinking with others (Mercer and Littlejohn, 2007).

For class teachers two important related ideas can assist us: these are collaborative learning and one means to harness this, dialogic teaching (Alexander, 2017a). Again, collaborative learning is more than learners simply tackling tasks together; it needs to be taught, for example, developing interpersonal skills. Collaborative learning can be articulated as the co-construction (Reznitskaya, 2012) of ideas. Individuals working together to, for example, clarify, apply, justify ideas and understanding. These words describe dialogue, which is much more than conversation.

Compare these short extracts, do they show thought? Reasoning?

Child 1 – My favourite number is 7.

Child 2 – I like them all.

Child 3 – 7's mine, too.

Child A – The biggest number of all is 100.

Child B – How do you know?

Child A – It's bigger than 99.

Child B – What's 99 + 10?

Child A – … Oh … that's bigger! It's 109.

The second extract shows how the learners' thinking has developed through the use of the question, How do you know? This question caused a chain of reasoning, which drew on some explanation, justification and refuting. The first extract could have easily led to some reasoning, but it stopped with the stating of a fact and the discussion around this.

One proven approach which aims to raise the quality of thinking through dialogue is dialogic teaching (Alexander, 2017a, 2017b). This idea recognises different kinds of talking but that two of them, discussion and dialogue, are less common in classrooms. Dialogic teaching supports learners and devotes time to having learners express, talk about and discuss ideas, then justify them, speculate and more, for example, making links and connections. One approach might be Mercer, Dawes and Staarman's (2009) talking points, where learners discuss ideas that are factually accurate, contentious or downright wrong.

REASONING FOCUS

Would these talking points lead to discussion?

Human pollution is bad for all life on Earth.

People cause all pollution.

Poorer countries should be allowed to pollute until they get richer.

People should not pollute the natural world.

Electric cars don't pollute.

You might also be familiar with *Concept Cartoons* (Naylor and Keogh, 2010) which also enable discussion.

REFLECTION

Language skills are essential to reasoning in mathematics and science, but they are important to all subjects. Can we apply these ideas across the curriculum? Can all subjects contribute to reasoning? In this way could the effect become cumulative?

The importance of metacognition

All thinking skills, including those we would recognise as reasoning, involve a degree of self-regulation. As this develops it contributes to self-awareness and thinking for oneself. We would advocate encouraging learners to think about their thinking, what Flavell (1979) called 'metacognition', for example, to reflect on how they learn best. While the skills outlined in this book begin with activities that support the teacher to help, model, question and direct learners, it is important to allow learners to develop their skills of reasoning independently, and without over scaffolding from the teacher. In fact, an over eagerness to support learners with reasoning may actually limit their opportunities to reason! One of the purposes of increasing learners' capacity to reason is for them to find structure or impose meaning on the problem they are trying to solve. Learners' reasoning will improve when they are allowed to think about their thoughts; we might encourage them to be self-reflective thinkers.

TRY THIS!

In lesson plenaries ask learners to reflect.

What have I learned? How will this help me in the real world? Can I use this in other subjects? Do I now think about things differently?

What do teachers think?

Before we examine where reasoning fits into the current English National Curriculum (DfE, 2014) you might first want to ask yourself if *you* think it does. We surveyed 44 primary teachers (Cross and Borthwick, 2017) about reasoning in the primary subjects. For them, mathematics – and to a slightly lesser extent, science – were the two subjects with the greatest potential for developing reasoning. Three other subjects (English, design and technology (DT) and history) were also selected by around one-third of the teachers. Other subjects such as PE, geography and religious education were identified by around one-quarter of the teachers. The 44 teachers appeared to have an understanding of the need for reasoning and some of the benefits it offered. One-quarter of them felt that reasoning is an innate skill, half felt it can be learned and one-quarter felt it was both innate and learned. Almost all were quite clear that primary-aged learners could reason and that reasoning began with preschool-aged children. When asked to select features of classrooms which enabled reasoning, about half the teachers selected open-ended questioning, child-led discussion and exploratory activity with around one-quarter selecting child-led activity, encouragement and acceptance of non-conventional answers. The options of closed questions and teacher-directed activity were each selected only once.

TRY THIS!

Why not survey your teachers/staff in school?

You can find the survey we used in Chapter 9.

When asked about reasoning itself, the teachers talked about thinking, deduction and problem-solving. They said that they value reasoning and feel that they can recognise it when they see it.

Almost all felt that professional teachers reason a great deal. But only a handful felt it was straight-forward to teach. They could suggest activities that would lead to learners reasoning and could identify opportunities for learners to reason. For some, reasoning was a form of directed thinking or thinking about a problem. They often talked about everyday examples of reasoning, for example, reviewing a diet.

We also asked a group of 38 student teachers (PGCE) to draw learners in a lesson where their activity had led to the children reasoning (Figure 1.3). Twenty-five of these drawings included mathematics activities, with five featuring science and the remaining eight featuring other primary subjects or general activities. All the drawings were plausible and regularly included learners working in pairs and groups. Other drawings showed learners talking to one another, or in some cases working alone. Speech bubbles suggested that lone learners were talking to themselves – what might be called inner-speech (Vygotsky, 1978). These examples all implied a cognitive engagement with a task, very often a problem-solving task. The illustrated learners were engaged with a task or context, were usually using or observing some form of equipment, had observed a relationship or phenomenon and appeared to be seeking a solution or explanation. There is a limit to what can be communicated in a drawing but the drawing activity and the discussion that followed provided useful reflection and even reasoning about reasoning. Student teachers felt that group work would be advantageous, that lessons should include time for learners to reason and that reasoning would often be stimulated by practical enquiry or engagement with a problem.

Almost all the student teachers found it challenging to suggest activities that would lead to reasoning, however all of them, working in pairs, managed to make several suggestions. They were less forthcoming when asked how to teach reasoning and struggled when asked about how learners' reasoning might develop progressively.

Figure 1.3 Student teachers' drawings of learners engaged in activities that led to reasoning

TRY THIS!

Ask learners or teachers to draw a picture of what it means to reason in mathematics or science.

Both teachers and trainees saw potential in mathematics and science for reasoning and could identify tasks and challenges which would enable reasoning; however, they were less confident when asked to suggest ways to teach reasoning.

REFLECTION

Is this an example of a learner reasoning?

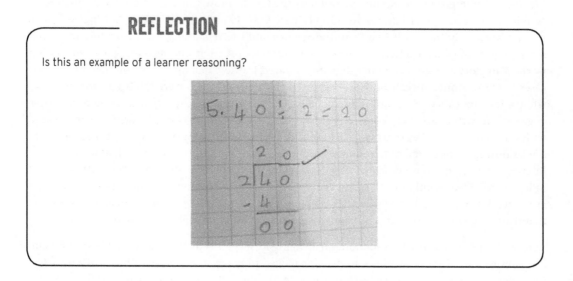

Where does reasoning fit into the English National Curriculum?

Reasoning is one of the core aims of the latest version of the English National Curriculum for mathematics (DfE, 2014):

> *The National Curriculum for mathematics aims to ensure that all pupils reason mathematically by following a line of enquiry, conjecturing relationships and generalisations, and developing an argument, justification or proof using mathematical language.*

> (DfE, 2014)

It is also included in the annual National Curriculum tests (STA, 2016a) that all learners aged 11 are required to sit (STA, 2016a). In the 2016 tests the question $5542 \div 17 = 326$ was included. Learners were asked to explain how they could use this answer to work out the following: 326×18. Only 33 per cent of learners across England were able to answer this correctly and 21 per cent did not even attempt the question.

Could it be that too much emphasis is placed on practising abstract questions which rely heavily on mathematical content, rather than teaching the **skills of reasoning**? Perhaps many learners looked at this question and assumed they had to calculate either a difficult division question, or a long multiplication question, rather than reasoning they could add 326 onto 5542?

Using reasoning skills to solve this question (e.g., pattern spotting, altering, making links) would have potentially resulted in more learners getting this question right than the 33 per cent who did. While learners need to show competencies in solving tricky calculations, they are rarely going to use them in real life (mobile phones usually include a calculator as one of the free applications). For this question, using reasoning skills would have made the question much quicker and easier to solve. Perhaps then, one suggestion as to why we should reason and teach the **skills of reasoning** is that if we do not, we are making the mathematics potentially more difficult than it needs to be.

While reasoning is one of the three aims, alongside fluency and problem-solving, in the English National Curriculum for mathematics, there are no specific objectives to support the teaching of reasoning within the yearly programmes of study. This makes it tricky for teachers to understand what reasoning looks like in each year group and within each mathematical area, let alone remember to include it. As we have already suggested earlier in this chapter, reasoning is key to the solving of problems. It is a skill which is essential to learners progressing with their mathematics, and so while it may not be as obvious as some of the more conventional mathematics we find in the curriculum (such as the learning of number facts or addition of fractions), it is arguably more important than the content provided.

In the English National Curriculum for science (DfE, 2014) there is no specific reference to reasoning, though there is mention of deeper understanding, abstract ideas and that science ideas change and develop over time. The non-statutory guidance contains references to forms of thinking, including analysing, exploring ideas, comparing and contrasting, researching, considering patterns, etc. While the term 'reasoning' is not used, it is clear that reasoning would enable the National Curriculum objectives and in particular what it calls working scientifically (DfE, 2014).

Learners appear able to gain knowledge in science, a strong feature of the English National Curriculum for science (DfE, 2014), but appear less able to use this knowledge. In a recent sample of testing in England learners were asked about candles burning in upturned beakers. After establishing that candles in different beakers are extinguished in different times, 11-year-olds were asked about a beaker twice the size and the effect this would have. Seventy-six per cent of learners gave a reasonable response, for example, doubling the time based on the information given. The remaining learners, while realising that the candle would burn for longer, made insufficient use of the information they had to deduce a reasonable conclusion (STA, 2016b).

Look at the example in Figure 1.4. What are you thinking? Are you reasoning?

As humans, most of us are full of ideas. Sometimes when there are a multitude of ideas it is hard to hold onto them and make sense of them. Using reasoning skills helps us to order these ideas, make sense of them and see the next steps in acting on them. When we reason we can use physical models, diagrams and research but we always have to engage with a context which often employs a question.

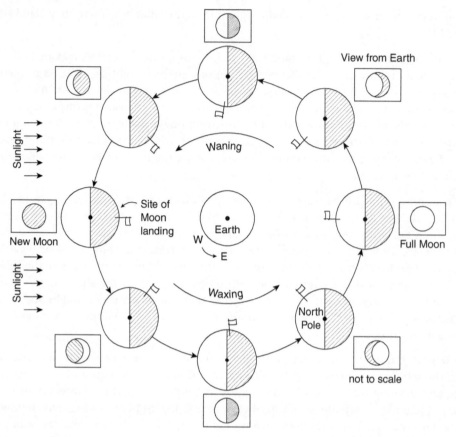

Figure 1.4 One side of the Moon always faces Earth, the other side gets equal periods of light and dark

REASONING FOCUS

The so-called 'dark side of the Moon' is never visible from Earth – so if you lived there would you ever see the Sun in the sky?

Find the solution in the Appendix.

Table 1.2 Chain of reasoning

Chain of reasoning	
About what is called the 'dark side of the Moon'	
I know the Moon orbits Earth.	Something I know.
I've read that the Moon spins (slowly in comparison to Earth).	A new idea to me.

I know only one specific half of the Moon ever faces Earth.	I remember this and suspect it may be linked to the answer.
Does that mean that all the Moon's surface experiences periods of light and dark?	I have a question which I think may help me.
So therefore, does the side which never faces Earth get as much light and dark as the rest of the Moon?	So this is another question.
So is this just the side we never see from Earth? It is just called the dark side but in truth it experiences 50% light and 50% dark just like the rest of the Moon's surface?	Does this question and this conjecture help me?

Would you recognise this as a chain of reasoned thoughts? It involves: recognising what I know; something I have noticed; something else I know which may be linked; another question; and a conjecture. Chapter 2 explores **skills of reasoning** further.

So, how might we teach learners to reason?

If we are going to teach reasoning, we first need to be able to recognise when learners appear to be reasoning. We asked teachers to imagine they were looking into a classroom. How would they know if the learners are reasoning? What would they be looking for or noticing?

Teachers said that learners might be:

- engaged in animated discussion;
- talking to each other;
- talking to the teacher;
- having a debate;
- disagreeing about something;
- using equipment;
- not writing in their books;
- appearing thoughtful.

Teachers said that learners would not be:

- working in silence;
- recording individually;
- disengaged;
- simply chatting;
- working passively.

┌─────────────── **REFLECTION** ───────────────┐

Do you agree/disagree with the above?

Could learners be working in silence yet still reasoning?

How would you know?

└──┘

We then asked the teachers, 'What would the teacher have needed to do to enable the learners to reason?'

The teachers said that teachers might have:

- given the learners a hook to spark their interest;

- been quiet, listening to the learners;

- posed a misconception or a mistake (perhaps it is written on the board?);

- organised the classroom furniture in a certain way (e.g., learners are sitting in a group or in a pair, or perhaps they are lying on the floor);

- provided learners with large sheets of paper to encourage group recording;

- asked the learners a question;

- encouraged questions from learners;

- begun a chain of reasoning and asked learners about the next step.

┌─────────────── **REFLECTION** ───────────────┐

Do you use any of the above?

What impact do they have on learners' reasoning?

└──┘

In writing this book we felt it was important to seek opinions from teachers and learners. Chapters 2 to 9 outline what we think are the skills of reasoning and offer ways to include these within lessons.

REFLECTION

What is your maths/science capital?

What maths/science do you know?

What do you know about teaching maths/science?

What is your attitude to maths/science?

What is your personal interest in maths/science?

What are your personal experiences of maths/science (in any form)?

Who do you know who knows, values, uses maths/science?

CHAPTER SUMMARY

This chapter has considered the reasoning we use in our everyday lives and how reasoning contributes to and is contributed to by primary mathematics and science. It has defined both thinking and reasoning and emphasised the importance of reasoning and the skills associated with reasoning. The chapter will have given you background and a flavour of what is to come in the book including ways we can reason and ways in which we can extend learners' thought with reasoning.

Having read this chapter you will:

- have considered definitions of thinking and reasoning;
- understand how thinking and reasoning are similar, yet different;
- be able to begin to identify **skills of reasoning**;
- have reflected upon the place of reasoning in at least two primary STEM subjects.

2
FRAMEWORKS TO PROMOTE REASONING

Introduction

Reasoning in mathematics and science is part of doing mathematics and science; perhaps the most important part. We can teach learners how to add numbers together, but do they really understand the concept of addition? They may be able to draw a food chain but are they appreciating how dependent organisms are on sunlight? To solve the problems that arise from everyday life we need to think and reason. This type of working is not about following a set of procedures or solving a familiar problem (both of which do have their uses in different ways and contexts). It is, for teachers, about how we spark curiosity in learners who may be used to thinking 'inside the box' when what we want them to do is to think 'outside the box' – and not only to think, but to reason.

We might assume that reasoning has featured in some primary classrooms for many years, but has it been actively taught or explicitly encouraged? Reasoning is used in everyday life and in occupations. In fact we can be certain that it is going to be part of the currency of the future. Development of reasoning in learning can contribute to, and is contributed to by, primary mathematics and science education. With clarity about what is meant by terms like 'thinking' and 'reasoning' (see Chapter 1) we feel that teachers will be better positioned to develop the **skills of reasoning** in learners and use this to ensure more progress and higher achievement in children's mathematics and science.

It is our intention that this book will have a positive effect on your confidence, skills and knowledge to teach reasoning in mathematics and science. We hope to do this by: (1) increasing your own knowledge and understanding of reasoning, for example, by exploring different **skills of reasoning**; (2) providing different frameworks for reasoning; and (3) increasing your toolbox of ideas for teaching reasoning in mathematics and science. This chapter explains what we mean by **skills of reasoning** and the different ways, including the use of frameworks, these can be used.

REFLECTION

What are your thoughts on the following?

Everyone can think. Everyone can reason. Teachers need to provide starting points and hooks for learners, to enable reasoning in different ways.

REASONING FOCUS

You will have realised by now that you are reasoning about reasoning – specifically about reasoning in primary classrooms. The clarity which we hope will come from this will assist you and is one very clear reason to reason.

Skills of reasoning

In Chapter 1 we distinguished between thinking and reasoning and provided a usable definition of reasoning. We concluded that reasoning is a form of thinking, in that it begins with thinking but also utilises skills such as justifying or proving, which makes the thinker think harder, order their thoughts and direct their thinking towards goal-orientated outcomes. We realised that although we often talk about these skills, we did not have a point of reference to go to which collects them altogether. Therefore, we and teachers we have worked with have considered, explored, discussed, tested and reflected on what these skills might look like (see Table 2.1).

This collection of the **skills of reasoning** is a starting point for you to explore within your teaching and with your learners. There will be others that we have not included and possibly ones that you do not agree with. We would encourage you to edit this list as you develop your own knowledge of the **skills of reasoning**. Many of these skills you will be familiar with. However, some may not be as obvious as others, or may contain levels of ambiguity towards their definitions, particularly as we are applying the skills to both mathematics and science contexts. Chapter 9 offers

Table 2.1 Skills of reasoning

convincing	working abstractly	decomposing	interpolating	evaluating
being logical	hypothesising	extrapolating	proving	predicting
deconstructing	generalising	speculating	explaining	agreeing/ disagreeing
questioning	noticing	describing	justifying	making connections
recognising links	being systematic	making judgements	pattern seeking	exemplifying
comparing	doing/undoing	organising	refuting	tinkering
correcting	altering	specialising	verifying	deleting
offering counter examples	visualising	working backwards	wondering	puzzling
classifying	observing	sorting	conjecturing	playing

a glossary of these definitions, through a reasoning lens, and also provides a mathematics and science example.

We believe that all of these skills are important in contributing towards reasoning. They are interdependent of each other and are therefore not hierarchical. In other words, one skill is not more important than another. However, it is fair to say that some of these skills are potentially harder to employ than others. For example, providing a counter example requires more cognitive thought than perhaps describing an activity or a process.

— TRY THIS! —

Give teachers a selection of the **skills of reasoning** and ask them to sort them, classify them, make connections between them.

It is worth noting that our list does not include specific mathematical or scientific skills such as calculating or measuring. We have deliberately not included these as **skills of reasoning**, as we would associate these elements within the subject-specific context of teaching the subject. We have also attempted to separate the **skills of reasoning** from the strategies for solving problems. Chapter 7 explores this further, but an example of a problem-solving strategy might be 'working systematically'. In order to work systematically learners may need to organise their work, notice patterns or make connections, all of which we suggest fall within the toolkit of reasoning. Without these skills we would suggest that learners may find solving problems tricky. As we have mentioned, we often use the **skills of reasoning** without realising. However, one of the purposes of this chapter is to be able to notice when we are using these skills so that we are alert to learners using them. In this way, we can identify strengths and gaps in reasoning so we plan and teach accordingly.

TRY THIS!

Could learners use these skills to review their own reasoning?

When discussing these skills with teachers, some have found it useful to include a selection in the front of learners' books or files. Learners then tally, date or tick when they believe they have been using one or more of the reasoning skills. Even if learners are quite liberal with their self-assessments, this type of activity raises the profile of reasoning and helps to makes it explicit and inclusive. An example is included in Table 2.2.

Table 2.2 Recording table for learners to note reasoning skills

	I used this skill in mathematics	I used this skill in science
convincing		
being logical		
noticing		
questioning		
recognising links		
comparing		
observing		
offering counter examples		
noticing		

One school used the idea of a checklist in learners' books but chose to include the reasoning skills within a problem-solving context.

Problem Solving Skill	Not Used	A Little	Conquered	My Teacher
Pattern Seeker				
Systematic Wizard				
Try & Improve				
Draw, Act & Use				
Reflection	What skills did you use to solve the problem? Was your strategy successful? Would you use a different one next time?			

Problem Solving Assessment

Problem Solving Skill	Not Used	A Little	Conquered	My Teacher
Pattern Seeker	✓			
Systematic Wizard	✓			
Try & Improve			✓	
Draw, Act & Use			✓	
Reflection	What skills did you use to solve the problem? Was your strategy successful? Would you use a different one next time?			

Figure 2.1 An example of a school's checklist

— TRY THIS! —

Choose five to six reasoning skills, collate onto a reasoning grid and stick in the front of learners' books/folders. Ask them to indicate both on the sheet and in their work when they think they have been using one of these skills.

A visual representation of the skills of reasoning

In exploring these **skills of reasoning** with teachers we noticed that a natural reaction was to begin to sort, organise and connect some of the skills together. Often this would depend on the activity or experiment at hand, as different skills are more useful and pertinent with specific tasks.

The examples in Figure 2.2 show how teachers sorted and organised some of the **skills of reasoning**, independently of a task. Notice how different teachers group different skills together, emphasising that there is no one correct way to view this.

*Figure 2.2 Examples of how teachers have organised, sorted and connected the **skills of reasoning***

We have also reflected upon using a visual representation of these **skills of reasoning** and a 'web of reasoning' seemed a useful image. In this example, **skills of reasoning** can be connected together in different ways. A web also suggests that all skills are useful, equal, and interdependent of each other, yet the web is only as strong as its weakest link.

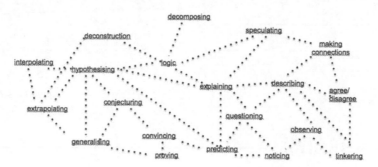

Figure 2.3 An example of a 'web of reasoning'

TRY THIS!

How would you draw a web of reasoning? Which skills would you connect together and why?

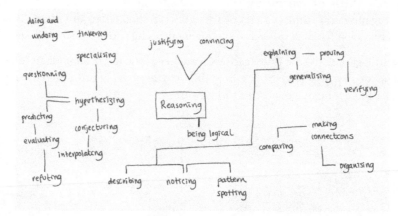

Figure 2.4 An example of a web of reasoning from teachers

Why do we need frameworks to help us to enable reasoning?

How teachers enable reasoning in learners is an area that requires some thought and exploration. This is because we need to be explicit about how we can enable reasoning within the classroom.

As professionals we require ways in which we articulate reasoning and ways in which we can think about reasoning as educators. In order to do this, we first need to understand what reasoning is (see Chapter 1); we then need to consider how we teach it so that we might enable learners to reason (Chapter 2); and finally, we need a bank of ideas and activities that we can use to facilitate reasoning (Chapters 3–7). With all of this in place, you, your learners and your school are heading towards engendering a culture of reasoning (Chapters 8–9).

Teaching reasoning can be employed in any one of a range of approaches, behaviours and contexts which we engineer in classrooms to enable specific learning. It may be useful to consider examples of such behaviours and approaches, such as:

- modelling reasoning;

- making reasoning explicit in lessons that 'we are/you are reasoning';

- designing tasks which require reasoning, e.g., conjecturing, hypothesising;

- making explicit use of associated skills, e.g., describing and explaining;

- giving examples of times when people have reasoned, e.g., Galileo, Archimedes;

- challenging learners with questions which ask Why? How? and Does this always occur?;

- asking learners to work in pairs or groups to help facilitate talk.

Such ideas are useful in classrooms. It is also helpful for teachers to consider frameworks that can guide their teaching and their design of lessons to develop learners' reasoning. There are, of course, many ways we can frame our teaching in order to promote reasoning. The purpose of this chapter is to allow you to become familiar with different structures and contribute to teachers reasoning about reasoning. The following chapters will then make reference to these frameworks and exemplify them through mathematical and scientific examples that you can try out in the classroom. You may find these frameworks helpful but you may also want to adapt, edit and refine them, according to your own bespoke needs. The stages we referred to in Chapter 1 enable all the features of the following frameworks.

Framework 1: Bloom's taxonomy

While it is hard to imagine school children not thinking, reasoning suggests a more purposeful, organised and goal-orientated skill. Perhaps it is reasoning which Bloom et al. (1956) and Anderson (2001) recognised as higher order cognition in aspects such as analysing, evaluation and creating? Whether he did or not, his taxonomy can provide a useful framework for us to consider how to promote reasoning within the classroom.

Bloom's taxonomy, named after Dr Benjamin Bloom who chaired the committee that devised the taxonomy (Anderson and Krathwohl, 2001), is a set of three models, one of which (Figure 2.5) describes the cognitive domain. The taxonomy is not hierarchical, but a statement about an interaction of skills. Remembering is not less important that understanding; they are both equally important but they are both essential before learners can really develop the skills of

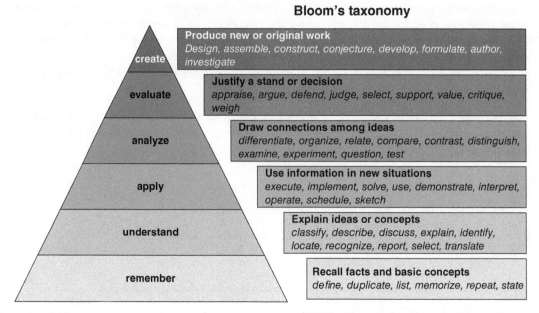

Figure 2.5 Bloom's taxonomy – cognitive domain

(Anderson and Krathwohl, 2001)

analysing and evaluating. The list we have included in Figure 2.5 refers to the cognitive domain (as opposed to the affective or psychomotor domains). It is also the 2001 revised model (which replaced *synthesize* with *create*). The revisions to the original taxonomy were thought to represent a more active form of thinking.

Bloom's model helps us to reason and think about different types of learning and complexity of thought. Much of the learning in primary classrooms may be around knowledge, comprehension and application. This learning can be extended and deepened where opportunities for analysis, evaluation and creation are exploited, for example, using what we have learned to hypothesise about and justify a mathematical or scientific idea.

The language which is associated with Bloom's levels can assist us as teachers to recognise and promote thought and behaviours associated with reasoning.

- Remember: the recall of facts and basic concepts. Within this level learners would be describing, identifying or recalling knowledge. Thinking is needed for this level but the skills we would recognise as reasoning are limited here.

- Understand: explain ideas or concepts. This level requires learners to show understanding, through explaining or providing examples. There is some reasoning required as learners begin to describe and explain.

- Apply: use information in new situations. At this level we would expect to see different **skills of reasoning** being used, for example, through learners being asked to tinker, alter or refute examples or thinking.

- Analyze: draw connections among ideas. This level begins to draw on those skills we would recognise as the connecting of ideas, or extrapolation of data.

- Evaluate: justify a stand or decision. This is a recognisable trait of reasoning as learners are required to justify, convince and use logic to support their evaluations.

- Create: produce new or original work. This final level utilises many **skills of reasoning** where learners need to harness the previous skills in order to create a new idea or example. This level could also use the knowledge of knowledge as well – in other words, metacognition.

As we began to look for and notice examples of reasoning in the classroom when gathering examples for this book, we were aware that although the teachers we spoke to were in favour of promoting reasoning, and could see the importance and value in it, many were unsure what it looked like or how to promote it. Often, reasoning would get lost within the world of problem-solving and the associated strategies.

Using a scaffold that many teachers have used previously, such as Bloom's taxonomy, may be a familiar way to explicitly consider the place of reasoning in the classroom. One of the advantages to using this framework is that it leans towards a focus on skills rather than content. The content (whether it is mathematics or science) is a vehicle for enhancing opportunities for learners to reason.

REFLECTION

Can you think of any lessons where you have promoted reasoning?

Which level of Bloom's taxonomy were exemplified?

Framework 2: NRICH 5 stages to reasoning

In their article 'Reasoning: the journey from novice to expert' (Pennant et al., 2014), the primary team at NRICH acknowledged that reasoning is *a complex business* and that learners need to understand and acquire skills such as systematic thinking and being able to communicate elegantly. In order to support the teaching of reasoning the team developed a five-step progression. While they recognise that learners may not move fluidly from one stage to another, it does provide some guidance towards the possible progression involved in reasoning. Like Bloom's taxonomy, the NRICH stages of reasoning are not hierarchical. All five stages are equally important but there is the notion that before learners can prove, they need to be able to explain or describe, for example.

While NRICH supports the learning of mathematics, these five stages are very applicable within a science classroom, too:

(1) describing

(2) explaining

(3) convincing

(4) justifying

(5) proving

'Describing' is the first stage and learners would simply be describing what they have done. For example, I added up the two numbers and got 20, or, I grouped the flowers according to colour.

'Explaining' is stage two and you would expect learners to be able to offer some reasons for what they did. These reasons may or may not be correct and their explanations might not yet be coherent at this stage. We would recognise this as inductive reasoning. For example, I sorted the numbers from smallest to largest so that I knew I had all the possibilities, or, It is important to clean your teeth so that your teeth don't fall out.

Stage three is 'convincing', and within this stage learners would be confidently offering some reasons, using phrases such as, 'without doubt' and 'I'm certain that'. You would expect to see some chain of reasoning at this level, but again it may not yet be accurate. However, in contrast to the previous stage you would expect to see more coherence and the reasons given more complete. Again this is inductive reasoning. For example, I am convinced that when I add an odd number to another odd number it equals an even number. While this is correct there is no justification as to why this is correct. Similarly, a science example might be, all metals are magnetic because I have tested three different metal objects and they are magnetic.

Within 'convincing' there are also different ways to convince. As Mason (1999) suggests, you can:

• convince yourself;

• convince a friend;

• convince a sceptic.

Each layer demands a slightly different skill. Convincing yourself is usually an internal, possibly silent, skill and you are rarely challenged on it! However, to convince a friend you need to enter into some explicit form of communication, either verbal or written. Once you begin to talk out loud or write down your reasons you often pause and consider your thinking and reasoning a little more than if you were convincing yourself. Finally, convincing a sceptic is perceived as the most challenging level. At this stage you need to be using some persuasive language or ideas, but of course you could still be wrong!

'Justifying' is the fourth stage and you would now expect a logical, correct chain of reasoning. Learners should be using words such as 'therefore' and 'because' and their chains of reasoning should be complete. For example, to divide by six, you can divide by three and then two, because three and two are factors of six, or, all mammals have warm blood and hair, therefore a whale is a mammal.

The fifth stage is 'proving'. Here learners are offering an argument that is correct and based on generalisations and an underlying mathematical or scientific structure. This is what we call deductive reasoning. Being able to prove (or disprove) something in mathematics is being able to construct a *complete and convincing argument to support the truth of an assertion, which proceeds logically from the assumptions to the conclusion* (Haylock, 2006). Proving follows on from generalising. To be able to prove something is an essential aspect of mastering mathematics and science. Proof in science, however, is a little different from proof in mathematics. In mathematics some things can be proven and as such will always exist in proven theorem. In science things are proved by observation in the real world. In science things remain proven until counter evidence is found. Thus, science theories always have the potential to be unproven by new evidence.

Being able to generalise and prove enables learners to begin to transfer their thinking. Often learners may have worked on one example initially. If they can then transfer their thinking to another example, and then another, they can move towards finding (or not) examples or structures that always work, which is the basis for a generalisation, and then finally a proof (Chapter 7 explores generalisation further). Seeking proof is a challenging skill and although it is one of our **skills of reasoning**, it is a particularly complex one – but one which all learners, regardless of age, can do.

There are different levels of proof, according to NRICH. For example:

- Proof by exhaustion: this level of proof depends on there being a small number of results so that it is possible to find all possibilities. This level is quite common in primary schools as it relies on children working systematically to ensure they have found all of the possibilities.

- Proof by counter example: this is where an example is offered that does not work and disproves the conjecture. This is sometimes known as 'proof by contradiction'. Learners can use a visual proof here, as well as an algebraic proof.

- Proof by logical reasoning: this is where the chain of reasoning is complete, there is no room for any gaps or ambiguities.

- Generic proof: this is where examples used allow the general structure to be noticed.

In science, proof is provided by observation, often within an investigation. The difference is that scientific proof can be disproved by a new observation. The NRICH levels of proof can help in science.

The NRICH five stages of reasoning are useful in exploring the different ways in which learners can reason. They allow us to see that there is more to reasoning than just giving a reason! Demanding a level of reasoning from learners allows them to begin constructing knowledge about the mathematics or science they are engaged with, rather than just exploring it in a casual, informal way. This type of approach prompts learners to think and reason, rather than just do. It allows learners to make sense of their mathematical and scientific experiences, so they can begin to construct and understand the structures behind the ideas they are engaged with – all of which provide opportunities for learners to reason!

─────── **TRY THIS!** ───────

Why not consider setting up a reasoning club in your school?

Framework 3: See, Think, Wonder

See, Think, Wonder is one of the techniques developed by Harvard University to help learners become better thinkers by providing them with thinking routines. As this book has suggested throughout, we need to teach learners how to think and reason. Good thinkers and reasoners have a toolkit of strategies to do this, but more importantly they use them! Researcher educators at Harvard University have been developing thinking strategies and they have developed several thinking routines, all designed to make thinking visible (Project Zero **www.pz.harvard.edu/projects/ visible-thinking**). Visible thinking is a systematic and flexible framework that supports learners with their thinking. It is thought that if we provide learners with a scaffold to think creatively, critically and deeply they will then begin to use these skills more often, perhaps when they begin to notice and question things. These habits or routines can be used with any artefact, question or phenomenon. The power in using one of these routines lies in its simplicity and structure:

- See – what do you see?

- Think – what do you think?

- Wonder – what does it make you wonder about?

The questions are asked in the order they are written and are therefore hierarchical in their pursuit to develop thinking and reasoning. For example, the first question is simply asking learners to say what they see. This is a very useful question to begin with as it encourages learners to stop and focus on whatever it is they are looking at. However, it also limits their answers to factual observations, rather than asking them to begin thinking and reasoning. The second question requires learners to begin thinking and also to offer some conjectures, hypotheses and predictions about what might be happening. We would expect to see some of the **skills of reasoning** beginning to appear here, for example, extrapolating data or explanations. Finally, the third question encourages learners to go beyond the object or picture and consider other factors. This question will potentially draw on different **skills of reasoning**, such as posing questions or making connections. Chapter 4 explores this pedagogical tool further using four pictures as the focus for the questions. However, we have included a mathematics and a science example (Figures 2.6 and 2.7) to support your thinking and reasoning about this framework.

We have also included a sample of the comments from a focus group of teachers.

What do you see?

- I can see lots of shapes.

- I can see triangles and hexagons.

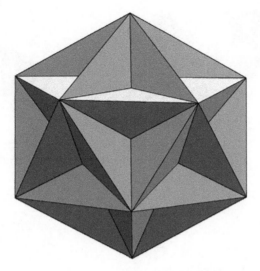

Figure 2.6 Giant dodecahedron

(Courtesy of Tarquin Publications **www.tarquingroup.com**)

- I can see pentagons.

- I can see both 2D and 3D shapes.

What do you think?

- I think there is reflective symmetry within the shape.

- I think I can see different types of triangles.

- I think different colours and shades will make up other shapes.

What does it make you wonder about?

- I wonder what the back of the shape looks like.

- I wonder if it is a 2D or 3D shape?

- I wonder what would happen if I tessellated the shape?

- I wonder if I would see all the shapes inside if I could only see the outline of the shape?

In a science lesson on the force of friction, Year 5 learners examined a climbing boot, a sledge and a skateboard. They were asked the See, Think, Wonder questions; we have included some responses.

Figure 2.7 Does friction help or hinder?

What do you see?

- I can see the plastic on the sledge is shiny.

- I can see the boot has a rubber sole so it has good grip.

- I can see the skateboard has wheels which will make it go fast.

What do you think?

- I think on a mountain you need a good grip or you will fall.

- I think the sledge must not have too much friction.

- I think the sledge won't go on the carpet.

- I think to go fast the skateboard and sledge have to have low friction.

- I think they all have friction.

What do you wonder about?

- I wonder is there a place with no friction?

- I wonder could I move without friction?

- I wonder is there friction in people?

- I wonder is there friction on ice? On snow? Under water? If you stood still?

These and follow-up questions led to interesting discussions about the difference between gravity and friction. The learners began to accept that friction would be found everywhere. They struggled with examples where friction is very low (for example, ice skating) and making a distinction between gravity and friction. The teacher found this very interesting and felt the 'See Think,

Wonder' scaffold had challenged the learners further. The teacher was keen to stress that often the best questions are not straightforward.

Framework 4: Using question stems

How? When? Why? Where? Who? What? are six typical questions we might hear and use in the primary mathematics and science classrooms. They are often used to check understanding but they can also act as a springboard to encourage learners to become aware of both the mathematical or scientific thinking processes, perhaps by suggesting conjectures and then moving onto exploration and investigation.

Chapter 4 provides subject-specific examples for each of these questions, but here are some sentence stems to give you a flavour.

How did you ...?

When would you ...?

Why does ...?

Where might you ...?

Who did ...?

What happens when/if ...?

While these questions are easy to use and plan for, they often focus on big fundamental concepts, partly because they are big questions! Using follow-up question stems might allow learners to focus more on details or smaller parts of what they are trying to think and reason through. For example: Does? Did? Can? Could? Might?

Does it make a difference if ...?

Did you consider ...?

Can you give me an example of ...?

Could you find ...?

Might there be another ...?

TRY THIS!

Put into place a 'reasoning action plan' to span across the year. Introduce a different framework every term or half term.

These question stems could be used as a framework in their own right, or as part of a way of supporting one of the other frameworks. Either way, using questions that elicit more than a one-word answer are beginning to invite learners to reason.

We hope that of the four frameworks described here, one or more may be meaningful and helpful to you. They might simply inform you, they might more directly influence elements of mathematics and science lessons, you might share some ideas directly with learners. You may not make extensive use of all four but you might find that one assists at this stage in your reasoning about reasoning.

CHAPTER SUMMARY

The purpose of this chapter is to consider what the **skills of reasoning** might look like. We have provided a list of words and phrases that mathematicians and scientists frequently use when they are reasoning. This chapter has also offered four different frameworks that we could use to support and scaffold reasoning in the classroom. Some of these frameworks may be familiar to you, yet you may not have considered their use in promoting reasoning, or the potential of making them explicit within your teaching.

Having read this chapter you will:

- have explored a range of skills associated with reasoning;
- have considered different frameworks to use to support reasoning in mathematics and science;
- understand how useful it is to make reasoning explicit within the classroom.

3
REASONING IN MATHEMATICS AND SCIENCE IN THE EARLY YEARS

— IN THIS CHAPTER —

By the end of this chapter you will:

- recognise opportunities for young learners to reason in mathematics and science;
- have considered ways to encourage young learners to think and reason;
- appreciate the diverse ways that young learners may reason.

Introduction

Why do the leaves fall?

What is the biggest shape?

How thin is thin?

Will extra wheels make this car go faster?

Is 100 the biggest number?

Questions like these have been asked many times by young enquiring minds, observing and think-ing about what they notice (Kallery, 2000). Such questions often appear naïve; the term naïve, however, can be misleading as such ideas offer practitioners valuable opportunities to challenge and excite learners about the world: their world. Such questioning provides practitioners with starting points for discussion, further experience and investigations. These questions often reveal miscon-ceptions. As we said elsewhere, misconceptions are valuable stepping stones for the learner towards greater understanding.

In England the Early Years Foundation Stage (EYFS) (kindergarden) curriculum (ages 0–5) is supported by materials such as *Development Matters* (DfE, 2012) and includes prime areas of personal, social and emotional development, communication and language, physical development and specific areas of literacy, mathematics, understanding of the world (which includes science), expressive arts and design.

The value of links between science and mathematics in the early years is recognised but may not be fully exploited (Vanstone, 2016). Here we consider reasoning in the two EYFS STEM areas, mathemat-ics and the scientific elements and understanding of the world. We will refer to the two subjects here though we realise the curriculum may be organised in different ways in different places.

Later sections of the book will also be relevant to Early Years practitioners as they consider impor-tant skills linked to reasoning and the **skills of reasoning**.

Young learners' mathematics and science

Mathematics in the Early Years is an exploration of the world and a growing understanding of measure, pattern and mathematical relationships which allows learners to perceive the world differently, to share ideas, think and reason about it using the amazing power of mathematics (Vanstone, 2016). From the play activity of bouncing balls, practitioners might encourage observations, questions, non-standard measures and recording to identify a relationship, for example, that the rubbery, flex-ible balls in our play area bounce the highest.

The literature around young children's science advocates child-initiated and teacher-led practical work, play, socialisation and talk (De Boo, 2006). This complements the work of Mercer et al. (2004) and Johnston (2009) who recognise the importance of talk to all learners. Another essential feature is that there is a strong exploratory element linked to confidence-building. Young learners need the opportunity and time to explore, often initially playing with new equipment like magnets or cubes. They need to feel that they are increasingly able to question and seek answers. They will need care-ful support so they are enabled to take the initiative, not be afraid of being wrong and happy to share thoughts and ideas about the world. De Boo (2006) recognises the place of reasoning by learners in Early Years settings.

How do young learners reason?

When young children observe everyday phenomena they will naturally ask how or why some-thing occurs. This questioning can annoy some adults as questions often come thick and fast; it can also be challenging as the questions can be tough and learners often expect adults to know all

TRY THIS!

Visit an Early Years setting and look at the displays and materials. Can you see evidence of mathematics and science? Can you see opportunities to develop the **skills of reasoning**?

the answers! A significant step in learning is that not all answers are known and even the youngest child can make discoveries; in fact they do on a daily basis. We do not want to stifle question-posing behaviour so we should see it as precious. At times we might even copy this behaviour!

Young learners can develop reasoning by observing, noticing, questioning, describing and wondering. They can do this alone but gain greatly from working and talking in pairs and groups (Crossland, 2015). Simply providing an answer will not give the child full opportunity. As literacy skills are variable and developing in young children, reasoning and thinking will require scaffolding by the teacher, who might be:

- assisting observation and noticing;

- asking learners to use more than one sense;

- encouraging learners to look for detail(s);

- being enthusiastic about learners' discoveries;

- accepting early ideas as learning opportunities;

- encouraging clarification;

- asking the learner to explain why they ask/say this?;

- encouraging questions;

- re-wording questions towards more mathematical or scientific questions;

- linking the learner's thought or question to another's;

- encouraging exploration;

- suggesting the learner explore different/other examples;

- asking the learner to suggest other observations – Here? Somewhere? Today? Tomorrow?;

- asking how others might assist us;

- encouraging use of equipment – for example, balls, toys, sliders, surfaces, lenses, musical instruments, etc.;

- encouraging deeper thought;

- suggesting identification of a possible question, prediction or challenge which can then be investigated;

- challenging with a counter view (perhaps by using a puppet);

- suggesting that another person might take a different view – What would they say?;

- using/encouraging open questions to enable thought – for example, Does that always happen? Why… ? When… ? Where… ?

Even young learners can ask deep questions which might include those we would recognise as philosophical. These are usually very genuine and can stimulate real thought, discussion and action in mathematics and science. They can then enable the **skills of reasoning**. They could include questions like these:

Are all animals friendly?

Why are there wasps?

How big is infinity?

What's the biggest number?

Is a triangle ever square?

Is the world big enough?

How high is high?

Why do stars twinkle?

Could a bird fly to the Moon?

What number is a sound?

Remember, in teaching reasoning the main objective is to reason, which we have said is a purposeful form of thinking; finding the right answer is desirable, but not our main objective. In a way the reasoning itself is the answer, or rather the thoughts and actions which follow. You can spend all day online looking for answers but a search engine is unable to reason!

Most EYFS environments are divided into areas and each should be considered to be potential contexts for reasoning in mathematics and science. Reasoning in the outside play area may start with noticing, observing and questioning – questions such as: Where do puddles go? Do worms sleep? How do birds keep warm? Is wet more slippery than dry? Which is the biggest container?

Reasoning in a wet play area could include questions such as: Which clothes are waterproof? Do fat buckets hold more water than thin ones? Is one big hole in a bucket worse than six small ones? How quickly can I pump this pot dry? How dry is dry?

Reasoning in the big apparatus area might offer opportunities to explore: Which shape makes the strongest house? How hard do we have to push to move this cube? How long does it take to build/dismantle a car?

Reasoning can occur in play areas, too. For example:

Is a triangle the best shape to make a frame for a tent?

Does dry or wet sand make the best sand sculptures? Why is that?

In what order do we add ingredients to a witches' brew?

Which material is best to build a shelter?

If we plant five seeds how many plants will grow?

Which food is most popular with birds?

Am I taller than this sunflower?

Recognising reasoning in EYFS

There is no doubt that young learners think and reason about the world and themselves. They may, however, not do this in a way which might be akin to that of adults. They tend to be delighted by new things, not threatened; they expect the world to surprise them. They might ask unexpected questions such as, Why is a bubble a bubble? It would be foolish to do anything other than take such a question very seriously. One young man is said to have once asked, Why does an apple fall? At the time this was considered by some to be a bizarre question.

REFLECTION

Can you recall your own early years?

Did you ask questions about the world?

What did you wonder about?

De Boo (2006) identified three areas of thinking and reasoning in the Early Years: creative and intuitive thinking; problem-finding and problem-solving; reflective and critical thinking. All recognise the considerable capacity of young learners to reason in so many ways, for example, wondering, puzzling, observing, noticing and more.

Reasoning in young learners may occur at lunchtime, at play, in the sand and water. It might be expressed in words but be manifested in movement or manipulation of materials. The practitioner's role is then to assist its development, in actions or into words. For example, shapes drawn in paint might range in size. Verbalisation might lead to more shapes, more sizes and a recognition of an order in size and to questions: What is the smallest circle we can paint? Is there another circle in there which is smaller?

Movement in play and drama may come before verbalisation. For example, children act out: she walked and then ran, walked and ran and ran, she ran on the path and walked in the wood all the way to grandma's house where she met the wolf. Who is she? How do we know? How could she have run quicker? What will she do now? The practitioner suggests going outside to look for places that are safe to run and ones where we might have to slow down. Different footwear is trialed to see why some is better suited than others.

Examples of contexts for reasoning in EYFS

Context for reasoning – bubbles

Young learners are fascinated by bubbles; their occurrence, production, appearance and characteristics. Allowing learners to play and then to explore can lead in all sorts of directions, including action and thinking.

Figure 3.1 Nursery-aged child trials water with four added spoonfuls of liquid soap

Figure 3.2 Children's own bent wire bubble blowers (teacher's writing)

Nursery-aged children were asked to observe bubbles in action (Figure 3.1). They were asked:

- What do you see? (circle, clear, shine, rainbow, round, a double bubble, a three bubble, a square bubble.)

- What do we make a bubble from? (water, soap/liquid soap.)

- How much water? (you need water … and soap.)

- Make your own bubble blower (Figure 3.2). What shape will the bubble be? (triangle, square, oval, love heart; one child draws an arch in the air, another says 'circle'.)

- How can we prove this is right? (we can make them and blow the bubbles.)

Figure 3.3 Nursery-aged children record how their bubble blowers worked

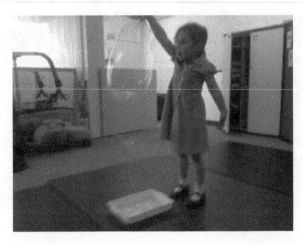

Figure 3.4 Can we make a bubble as tall as we are?

These young learners needed to show others and talk about their discoveries; they were encouraged to record, often preferring to do this pictorially (Figure 3.3). All of the learners were then intrigued by bigger and bigger bubbles. This led to the questions: Can we make one as tall as you are? How? Can you explain? Can you show me?

REFLECTION

Have you wondered about bubbles?

Why are they transparent close up, but yet bubbles in a bath look white?

Context for reasoning – 2D shapes

In this classroom (Figure 3.5), learners explored how to make different shapes using only triangles. They explored how to put triangles together in different ways and whether they were the same or different.

Figure 3.5 Learners reason why their combinations of triangles are different

While these learners explored triangles, any 2D or 3D shapes are opportunities for enabling children to reason, and in turn develop thinking in geometry. When exploring shape remember to use atypical shapes too, so that learners use their skills of reasoning to justify why a triangle is a triangle. Often, learners will decide that the triangle below is not a triangle (see Figure 3.6). They are not reasoning about their answer, simply using previous reference points to assist their thinking.

Figure 3.6 An atypical representation of a triangle

Context for reasoning – bones

These learners were exploring parts of the body while the teacher was linking this to a number of science and other PSHE themes.

Figure 3.7 Reception-aged learners examine the bones of a sheep

Reception-aged learners were intrigued by real sets of bones (Figure 3.7) which they handled and observed. They immediately began to notice features: 'The eye went there'; 'What is that line?'; 'Why is there a hole there?'; 'Why are the teeth wobbly?'; 'Is this part of that?'; 'Why is it white?/ yellow?'; 'It's got no front teeth!'; 'What's that (the nasal cavity)?'

Other questions posed were: 'Is it a real one?'; 'How did it die?'

The learners were told that these were real bones and had been found on the side of a mountain in Wales. Asked about the animal, they suggested it might be, 'a giraffe', 'a goat' or 'a dog'. Asked why they thought this they reasoned that, 'It has horns', 'I've seen a giraffe ... at the zoo'.

One learner asked how the animal died. This question was put to the group and suggestions included, 'it bumped into a wall', 'it was in a fight with a dog', 'it fell off ...'. This led to a long discussion about what might have happened.

Asked to fit the bones together, the learners pushed the sets of teeth together explaining, 'these go here', 'it needs two', 'it can eat things now'.

TRY THIS!

Visit an Early Years setting and talk to learners while they play. Given a question, will they go a little deeper with, Why? How? Could? Would?

Context for reasoning – the playground

Lots of children love learning outside. So, why not take out the chalk and some mathematics equipment and let them explore? In Figure 3.8 learners explored number patterns with their Numicon tiles.

Playground mathematics (and science) is rich in opportunities for learners to be creative and to experiment with their ideas (Cross and Board, 2015). As a practitioner, notice when learners are using the **skills of reasoning**. Are they being logical? Sorting? Wondering? Tinkering?

Context for reasoning – stories and tales

Early Years practitioners know the value of stories and themes for initiating and sustaining learning; they are ideal for reasoning.

Funnybones: Why do we have bones? Do all animals have bones? What are bones like? Do babies have bones?

Handa's Surprise: How many kinds of fruit are there? Why is fruit healthy? What is the biggest banana?

365 Penguins: How big is a penguin? Can they fly? Why do they swim? Do they get cold? Why not? Can we count them?

Figure 3.8 Learners use the playground to explore number patterns with Numicon

Foggy Foggy Forest: Who is in the forest? Why are they there? What will they do? Why can't we see them clearly?

One is a Snail Ten is a Crab: What number comes next? Is there a pattern? Could we have a different combination of feet to make up this number?

How Big is a Million?: Have you ever seen a million? What is the biggest number you know? Do you think a million stars will fit onto one piece of paper?

The Enormous Turnip: Why was the turnip so big? How did it grow? Can we pull things? Can we do little pulls and big pulls?

Jack and the Beanstalk: How high was the beanstalk? Does it reach the clouds? Can we grow a giant beanstalk?

The Little Three Pigs: How strong is a house? Can we blow things over? How does blowing move things? Can we make a strong house?

Context for reasoning – themes

The seaside: Where is the seaside? What's in a rockpool? Why do some animals have shells? Which is the smallest animal that lives in the sea?

Minibeasts: How far can a woodlouse walk? What does an ant think? What does a spider eat? How can we sort minibeasts? How many are there?

Pondlife: How deep is the pond? Is it safe? Is there a shark? What would we find at the bottom?

Under the sea: What is a shipwreck? Do fish sleep? Can people go under the sea? How deep is it?

The high street: How tall is a door/sign/shop? Which shops do we find? Could we get lost? Do pets like shopping? Do all shops want money?

Encourage learners to make up their own stories, too. For example, perhaps some learners could make up a story for the number three? They might like to use some resources to help them explain, and perhaps even act out their number story. How does it become three? If it starts at three does it become two, then one, then zero? Activities such as this one encourage learners to reason but also strengthen the links between how we represent numbers – both in a concrete and an abstract way.

Context for reasoning – play areas

Play areas might include: café; farm; doctor's surgery; fire/police/bus/railway station; vet's; or shop.

In each play context apply questions such as:

What do we wear in the …? Why?

Who comes here …? Why do they?

What do grown ups do here?

What do children do here?

What happens here …? What happens next?

Is there a … nearby? Far away? Would it look the same?

What would a … look like on the Moon?

All these contexts exemplify the findings of Gatt and Theuma (2012), who found that stories were effective vehicles in science as the learners associated themselves with the characters in the story. Practitioners will see the potential also for mathematics. The stories provided a purpose for carrying out the investigations, leading to meaningful discussions. Help learners link between scientific concepts and the real world. Learners had no difficulty switching from the fictional story to the non-fictional investigation.

Further to the examples above are several more below, where in each case we note **skills of reasoning** which might be developed.

— TEACHING ACTIVITY —

Skills of reasoning: noticing, questioning, observing, tinkering, puzzling, hypothesising

Figure 3.9 Examples of noisy toys

If you provide your learners with a collection of noisy toys can they explore them? Identify any parts that move? Say how the noise is made? Say how we hear this? Can they think of ways to make a noisy toy quieter?

— TEACHING ACTIVITY —

Skills of reasoning: wondering, noticing, generalising, speculating, observing

Figure 3.10 A seedling

In your garden area or an indoor planter, can you plant one sunflower, two bean seeds, three beet-root seeds, four tomato seeds and five pea seeds? Could learners care for them? Say what will happen? Observe the seedlings (and others you might sow)? Describe what happens? Measure them (in bricks)? Model them? Ask how do things grow? Ask is this how we grow?

TEACHING ACTIVITY

Skills of reasoning: noticing, making judgements, observing, predicting, generalising

Figure 3.11 Examples of different types of materials

In a play area could learners play with materials to slide down a mini slide? Could they say what happens? Can they talk about other slippery things? About things that rub? Can they say what would happen if we wet the material a little? Can they record? Can they describe the materials that are slippery?

TEACHING ACTIVITY

Skills of reasoning: sorting, comparing, describing, organising, grouping and classifying

Figure 3.12 Coloured rods

Give learners a pile of coloured rods. Can they sort them? Order them? Describe them? Explain?

── TEACHING ACTIVITY ──

Skills of reasoning: sorting, convincing, explaining, organising

Give learners lots of different resources. Ask them how many ways can we make 3? 4? 7? 12?

Examples of resources could include:

piles of sticks

conkers or pebbles

plastic cubes

Numicon tiles

shells

plastic dinosaurs, bears, beads, fish

Can they convince you that 4 is 4? Or 7 is not 8?

Ask questions such as:

How did you make 12?

Is there another way?

How many other ways are there?

Can you explain why?

── TEACHING ACTIVITY ──

Skills of reasoning: comparing, convincing, proving, puzzling, working backwards

Who has the most? Who has the least?

Ask learners to take a handful of counters or cubes. Ask them who has the most. This activity helps learners to think about the size of numbers, offers them opportunities to compare numbers and also uses their reasoning skills to convince each other, or otherwise!

Figure 3.13 Counters and cubes

TEACHING ACTIVITY

Skills of reasoning: noticing, observing, describing, wondering

What is the same? What is different?

We have used this question frequently throughout the book to enable learners to reason, and younger children are just as able to respond to this question as older learners.

Ask learners to choose their favourite number or shape.

Then compare two or three of the numbers or shapes.

What is the same between the numbers? Shapes?

What are the differences?

3

TEACHING ACTIVITY

Skills of reasoning: noticing, proving, sorting, organising

21   2   12   1

Asking learners to notice is a key **skill of reasoning**. But our number system is complicated and often difficult to understand. Look at the four numbers above. Learners may find it tricky to notice the difference between 21 and 12, for example. Ask learners to show you what these numbers look like using resources (e.g., using counters or shells). Can they spot the differences? Which is the biggest number? Smallest number? Are they sure? Which number do they think will have the most counters in it? Why?

TEACHING ACTIVITY

Skills of reasoning: noticing, pattern seeking, describing

Give learners a pattern to copy - either a practical one that you have made from cubes, counters or plastic animals, or a picture of a shape.

Notice how they copy the pattern. Do they copy the colour? The size? The quantity?

─────── **CHAPTER SUMMARY** ───────

This chapter has shown that rich Early Years settings are crammed with opportunities for young learners' reasoning. Practitioners are usually very good at exploiting meaningful contexts for young minds and the ideas in this chapter and book will assist you to further exploit activities and contexts to develop the **skills of reasoning** and recognise them as they develop. A critical message is that young learners can, and do, reason often with impressive clarity!

Having read this chapter you will:

- recognise opportunities for young learners to reason in mathematics and science;
- have considered ways to encourage young learners to think and to reason;
- appreciate the diverse ways young learners may reason.

4
USING QUESTIONS TO PROMOTE REASONING

--- IN THIS CHAPTER ---

By the end of this chapter you will:

- know that all questions are useful;
- be clear about how questions in the classroom can lead to learners reasoning;
- have considered a wide range of different types of questions;
- have a developing toolkit of teaching approaches that all use questions to enable reasoning;
- know why questioning is one of the **skills of reasoning**.

Introduction

This chapter will ask you to reflect on the use of questions in the classroom in order to promote reasoning. It will encourage you to challenge the current use of questions in classrooms and suggest that the focus of questioning moves towards the children. Learners who are confident to question, who are not anxious about the need to find the right answer, who make use of questions in their learning and are less willing to rely on others for answers, are developing skills we would recognise in mathematicians and scientists. Using questions is one of the ways we enable **skills of reasoning**.

In the Appendix we offer a toolkit that collates and organises different types of questions that you may find to be a useful rubric to enable learners to reason.

Why are questions important in supporting reasoning?

While teaching methods may change and develop over time, the use of questions to elicit knowledge and scaffold learning remains at the heart of much teaching and learning. Whatever the latest persuasion, (e.g., 'mastery teaching'), asking questions is still at the core of good teaching and learning. Questions feature in all classrooms, for example, questions asked by adults, questions asked by learners (though there are rarely enough of these), and questions posed or prompted by media such as books, applications, film and animations. Powerful though questions can be for learning, they can be used inefficiently and so lose much of their potential. For example, while there is a place for closed questions such as 'How tall is she?', open questions can offer more in terms of getting learners thinking and reasoning, such as, 'Is she an average height for her age?' The second question is still focused on the same piece of knowledge, but now it has extended the thinking by demanding an answer where the learner has to begin to connect ideas and explain the reasons for their answer. In this example, reasoning is required to pose and to answer this question. However, as the examples in this chapter will show, it can also be the way a question is used, as opposed to the type of question it is (e.g. open or closed) that encourages learners to draw on their reasoning skills.

To be a mathematician or scientist you need to be active in thinking about and doing mathematics and science. Asking questions and using **skills of reasoning** help to support you as a mathematical and scientific thinker, rather than just accepting the facts and applying the procedures.

Mathematics and science require questions, but not those questions so often heard in classrooms, for example, 'What is 3 + 4 ?' or 'Name three bones in our bodies?' The sort of questions this chapter considers are those which are driven by curiosity, that require the learner to connect ideas, sort the information and do something with their thinking. For example, 'Can I make a parachute that is dropped from two metres and always hits its target?' or 'If I increase the perimeter of a shape will the area always increase too?' These types of questions provide a starting point for exploration and reasoning.

The former, simpler questions often require a function to be selected and carried out. The latter questions foster mathematical and scientific thinking because they provide learners with experiences through which they can build rich connections. Knowledge should not only be treated as consisting of distinct parts. It is perhaps the difference between 'doing' mathematics or science and 'knowing' about some aspects or elements of mathematics or science.

We could apply such questions to the pictures in Figure 4.1. Have I seen anything like this before? What might be the ingredients? Did the ingredients look anything like this product? Could we change the ingredients? Are all the products visible to the eye?

Another example may assist. If you ask, 'Could humans travel to a star?' you need to clarify what a star is and whether there is one nearby (the closest, after the Sun, is Proxima Centauri – 4.3 light years away (**www.bbc.co.uk/news/science-environment-37167390**). Then, we need to consider how far is that in kilometres or miles? (9.5 trillion kilometres or 5.9 trillion miles.) Thus, we move through a series of questions to deduce if this journey is possible. Once we know that the speed of light is around 300 million metres per second we come to a point where arithmetic will tell us how many years it would take, travelling at the speed of light, to get there. Our rockets only travel at 20,000 miles per hour so it would take 137,000 years. Many, many generations of astronauts would

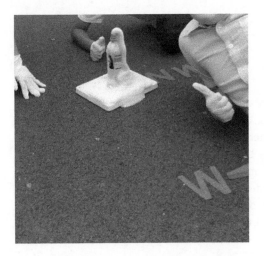 

Figure 4.1 A primary science club posed questions about 'Elephant's Toothpaste'

(hydrogen peroxide (weak concentration), food colouring, liquid soap, yeast and water)

live and die on this journey! So, new questions might then be posed. What kind of vessel would enable this? Would the humans on board evolve into a new species on the journey? In order to answer this question ('Could humans travel to a star?') we have needed to 'know' some mathematics and science, but we have also needed to 'do' something with this knowledge, which in this case was to recognise the types of questions to ask to pursue the problem.

REFLECTION

Do teachers ask too many questions?

Are there types of questions that are more powerful than others to enable reasoning?

Connecting mathematics and science through questions

There are many ways that mathematics and science are connected, for example, through the use of data, quantitative values, measures, pattern, proportion (Cross and Borthwick, 2016). Using questions to support reasoning is a particularly strong link. Posing questions allow us as teachers to:

- find out what children know or don't know;

- probe their understanding further;

- stimulate interest and curiosity;

- scaffold learning;

- extend their thinking into reasoning.

Many of the questions that these two subjects ask are connected through their exploration to work mathematically or scientifically (Cross and Borthwick, 2016). It is within this area in particular that the two subjects have significant crossover, yet learners often view these subjects as being separate and discrete. While mathematics and science remain their own separate 'pillars of human thought and creativity' (Cross and Borthwick, 2016), there is an increasing persuasion to connect and unite mathematics and science so that learners can become equally informed individuals in both disciplines (The Royal Society, 2014). The types of questions that each subject might draw on to enable reasoning are common to both, and it would be hard to distinguish between whether the question stem is more mathematical or scientific.

TRY THIS!

In your next mathematics/science lessons, make very explicit links to maths/science.

Can the learners explain the link?

The range of questions that we have included in this chapter go beyond simply the selection and process of information needed to reach an answer. They tap into learners' curiosities by asking the questions they are interested in, not just the questions they have to ask and answer to pass tests. They help to support a mathematically and scientific-literate workforce by encouraging learners to think and reason so they have the ability to formulate and solve complex problems in the future, often with others. As the National Council of Teachers of Mathematics (NCTM) wrote, *businesses no longer seek workers with strong backs, clever hands and 'shopkeeper' arithmetic skills* (NCTM, 1989). These questions help learners to become mathematically and scientifically powerful by encouraging them to explore, hypothesise, conjecture and reason. Of course, being able to draw on mathematical and scientific subject knowledge is important and necessary in moving between thinking and reasoning. The ability to make sense of a problem, to become confident in your own ability to think and then reason, to be a problem-solver and to learn to communicate mathematically and scientifically, are skills where exposing learners to different types of questions can promote and increase their **skills of reasoning**.

In both subjects, learners are presented with problems to solve. While they will need to draw on specific subject content knowledge, the way they examine and dissect the problem is very similar. They might start by asking questions and using prompts from the following selection:

What is ...?

Have I seen this before?

Can I do it this way?

Does ... always occur?

Can I explain ...?

Is there a pattern?

What sources would help me account for this?

If I do ... what will be the effect?

Do I know something similar which will help?

I don't know but it might be ...

I noticed that ...

From these questions it is impossible to decide if the problem is mathematical or scientific. However, teachers of both subjects will recognise that these questions are present in both. To support the mathematicians and scientists of the future we need to show them that neither subject is just about a fixed set of concepts and skills; they are not spectator sports, but subjects that learners can discover, engage with and enjoy. Using questions is one way to do this.

REFLECTION

Consider how you use questions when teaching science and mathematics.

Different types of questions

The following section offers different types of questions that both subjects can utilise in order to enable learners to think and then reason. While we would value all questions, there are particular, desirable characteristics that help to enable **skills of reasoning** that other questions have limited capacity to do. ACME (2016) for example, offers a list of question characteristics that could be used to assess problem-solving:

- varying the presentation (to avoid predictability);

- making choices (choosing an appropriate method);

- thinking mathematically (probing closely related variants of the original question);

- obtaining results (solutions have to be interpreted and communicated and sometimes rejected in preference to another);

- making modifications (making variations or changing assumptions).

In Chapter 1 we discussed how reasoning is a critical element of problem-solving and so the list ACME offers is both worthwhile and essential to this book. However, within this chapter we have tried to choose particular questions that are specifically drawing on reasoning skills, rather than the broader area of problem-solving.

In many cases the types of questions presented are actually a 'question stem'. By this we mean the first part of the question is offered, but the last section needs adding to. This is often where the subject-specific part is defined.

It is also useful to name different types of questions because the label can be easily recalled, which is helpful when planning mathematics or science lessons. We have used some very recognisable labels, which did not originate with us, but have been frequently used over the years in both subjects. You may wish to change the label and replace it with one of your own and, of course, we would encourage you to add to this list too! The questions are powerful in enabling reasoning because they are prompts for learners to begin thinking. They provide a starting point for thinking and discussion, which can then lead to more logical, organised and systematic thoughts that we would begin to recognise as reasoning.

However, while the question stems that follow provide an excellent starting point to enable reasoning, they are only the beginning. It is really the conversation or discussion that follows which is a powerful opportunity to capture and develop children's reasoning. This is very difficult to show in a book (see Chapter 8 for how to evidence reasoning), and so we offer these question stems as a starting point for these discussions to begin.

1. Can you give an example of ...?

This is a powerful question to ask because it starts with a generalisation that learners then need to provide specific examples for. Once learners have offered an example, you can then ask for another, and another. As more examples are generated, so too are the **skills of reasoning** as children are asked to convince and justify their responses. To begin with, learners will often give the first example that comes into their head. But by asking for more examples different skills are drawn out. For example, learners may begin to think systematically, consider more complex examples and even offer some generalisations. While this question begins as a closed question, it is the pursuit of more answers that opens out the range of possibilities and thus encourages learners to go beyond one answer, and to begin to think more deeply.

Finally, you can ask what is common to all of the responses.

TEACHING ACTIVITY

Skills of reasoning: noticing, pattern spotting, specialising, explaining

Can you give an example of a pair of numbers whose sum is 4?

Initial answers could include: $0 + 4$; $1 + 3$; $2 + 2$.

However, if we now follow these answers with the question 'and another?' it can enable some different thinking.

Answers could now include: $5 + -1$; $6 + -2$; $10 + -6$.

So, although the first answers all used whole numbers, learners may now be exploring the addition of negative numbers. This question type has extended the learning and probably depth of thinking. Learners began by describing simple equations, but have now moved on to explaining and convincing others about more complex sums.

Can you give an example of an object which is magnetic?

Initial answers could include: a paperclip; 1p or 2p coins; nails.

Extend to other examples familiar and less familiar?

Our noticing might extend to ask why some metals are magnetic and others not.

Using these types of questions enables learners' thinking and reasoning to naturally extend with very little prompting.

2. What do you notice?

Earlier (see Chapter 1) we emphasised the importance of noticing. Noticing can be a pre-cursor to some cognitive activity. It is more than 'seeing', as it is a way to facilitate the connecting of ideas and thoughts together. To begin with, noticing could simply be in the form of stating facts, but as learners begin to notice more, they may begin to ask questions and connect ideas together. They are now moving towards utilising **skills of reasoning**.

TEACHING ACTIVITY

Skills of reasoning: noticing, pattern spotting, describing, questioning

Look at this pattern.

1	2	3	4	5	6	7	8	9	10
11	12	13	14	15	16	17	18	19	20
21	22	23	24	25	26	27	28	29	30
31	32	33	34	35	36	37	38	39	40
41	42	43	44	45	46	47	48	49	50
51	52	53	54	55	56	57	58	59	60
61	62	63	64	65	66	67	68	69	70
71	72	73	74	75	76	77	78	79	80
81	82	83	84	85	86	87	88	89	90
91	92	93	94	95	96	97	98	99	100

Figure 4.2 An example of a hundred square

What do you notice?

What questions do you want to ask?

What will the next shaded number be?

How do you know?

Is there a pattern?

In a mathematics lesson, learners were given squares, which they had to colour in half. Each time, learners had to record their findings in a chart. The task began with one square (half a square coloured in), then two squares (one square coloured in), three squares (one-and-a-half squares coloured in), and so on. After the learners had explored the task, the teacher asked them what they had noticed. One Year 4 child, aged 9, said, 'I noticed that the first number got halved as it got to the end of the chart and it goes like this, ½, 1, 1 ½, 2, 2 ½, and so on. 1 if you half it you get ½.' (Figure 4.3).

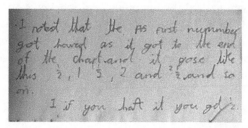

Figure 4.3 A Year 4 child notices a pattern in number

The child is beginning to recognise a pattern. The teacher then went on to ask what if you had 10 squares, 20 squares, 100 squares? Answers from the class included, 'If you multiply the original number by 4 and then divide by 2 you get the answer' (9-year-old).

While this is not (yet) correct, it is not important in this context. The significant point is that the child is having a go, beginning to spot patterns and beginning to use the **skills of reasoning**, because they are looking for patterns and trying to describe and communicate their ideas.

Look at this diagram of a food web.

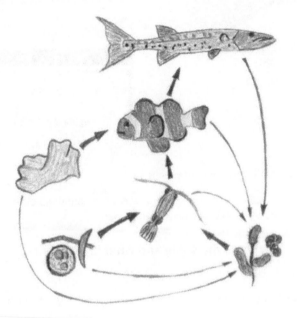

Figure 4.4 An example of a food web

(Image from Wikimedia Commons)

What do you notice?

What questions do you want to ask?

3. What is the same and what is different?

This question encourages learners to look closely at the examples given and to notice both the similarities and the differences in both.

TEACHING ACTIVITY

Skills of reasoning: describing, explaining, making connections, extrapolating

Look at the two charts.

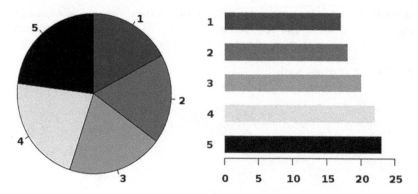

Figure 4.5 A pie chart and a block chart

(Image from Wikimedia Commons)

What is the same and what is different between them?

In the example in Figure 4.6 a class was asked, What is the same and different between the two 3D shapes? Their answers were recorded on the whiteboard.

What is the same and what is different?

Cube-edges are the same size

Cube is equilateral, everything is
equal but the cuboid is not

Same in every way but the
cuboid is longer

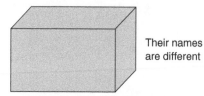

Their names
are different

Both got 24 right angles

Same colour

Both got 12 edges

Every edge is parallel to another edge

Both got 8 vertices

The cube if higher so the cuboid is lower

Same amount of faces but the faces aren't
the same size in the cuboid

Figure 4.6 Same or different?

Notice how the learners focus on the properties of the two shapes, spotting properties such as parallel lines, vertices, angles and edges. It is a simple question to ask but it immediately encourages learners to begin to organise information and connect ideas. At the moment these learners are using **skills of reasoning** such as describing and explaining, which is enabling them to begin to reason about the similar and different properties between a cube and cuboid.

Look at the different circuits.

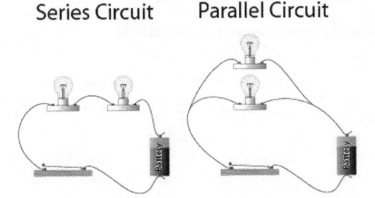

Figure 4.7 A series and a parallel circuit

(Image from The Science Classroom Wikispaces)

What is the same and different between them?

4. Which is the odd one out?

This type of question encourages learners to offer reasons why one of the examples could be the odd one out. If the examples are chosen carefully, any one of them could be the odd one out! The very nature of this type of question lends itself to reasoning, as a simple answer without a 'because' will not be sufficient. This is an example of a closed question, which encourages reasoning because of the examples it is attached to.

TEACHING ACTIVITY

Skills of reasoning: speculating, convincing, explaining

Which number is the odd one out?

1, 7, 12

1.4, 364, ¼

(Continued)

(Continued)

Which planet is the odd one out?

Earth, Mars, Saturn

Venus, Mercury, Uranus

Different examples draw on different **skills of reasoning**.

Skills of reasoning: comparing, refuting, exemplifying

Which calculation is the odd one out in each set of three?

$2 \times 10 = 20$
$21 \times 10 = 210$
$200 \times 10 = 200$

$2/5 + 3/5$
$6/4 - 2/4$
$4/13 + 8/13$

Which object is the odd one out?

a wooden spoon
a pebble
a twig

5. Is this always true, sometimes true, or never true?

This type of question often starts by posing a statement, which learners are then encouraged to find examples for that either show the statement is true or offer counter examples to illustrate it is not. Dillon (1985) has shown that learners often respond better to talking about a statement rather than answering a question. This is because statements can lead to more dialogue, a higher involvement from more learners and richer discussions or arguments! Statements can appear to be more conditional and therefore invite learners to make meaning from them, as opposed to questions which are often seen as a test.

TEACHING ACTIVITY

Skills of reasoning: generalising, specialising, offering counter examples

Are these statements always true, sometimes true, or never true?

Multiplication always makes numbers bigger.

There is an eclipse every year.

All numbers in the 4 times table end in a four.

Plant material comes from the soil.

If you increase the perimeter of a shape, the area also increases.

Sound travels in straight lines.

6. Can you give an example of a peculiar, an obvious and a general example?

This question, sometimes referred to as a POG, encourages learners to both generalise and specialise because it is asking children to provide examples on the same piece of knowledge.

As with many of the other questions, the examples are only as powerful as the reasons learners give to justify their choice and are open to many different interpretations. However, by asking for a range of answers on the same mathematical or scientific area, learners begin to seek more complex examples and the expectation to provide a general example can lead learners into considering in what way an example is generic.

TEACHING ACTIVITY

Skills of reasoning: generalising, specialising, justifying

Can you give an example of an even number?

Peculiar: 7,392 (because the other digits in the number are odd, except the digit in the ones column).

Obvious: 2 (because it is the smallest even number).

General: any whole number which, when divided by 2, has no remainder (a definition of an even number).

Can you give an example of an object that conducts electricity?

Peculiar: Graphite in a pencil (because it has electrons that can move; it is, however, a poor conductor of electricity).

Obvious: Steel object (because it is used in wires; however, some metals are very bad conductors of electricity, e.g., stainless steel).

General: Metals conduct electricity (yes they do, but some are very poor conductors of electricity).

7. If this is the answer, what is the question?

These types of questions are fun to ask and in our experience children love them! Learners often assume that the point of a question is to discover the answer. Yet if the answer is the starting point, a different approach is needed to end at the beginning. The following questions encourage learners to consider different possibilities, as there could be many questions that could result in the same answer. These types of questions offer learners the opportunity to draw on different **skills of reasoning** as they begin to work systematically, sort and organise the information and consider the range of possibilities. They may even begin to offer generalisations if they can spot patterns in the answers they are finding.

TEACHING ACTIVITY

Skills of reasoning: working systematically, organising, pattern spotting, deconstructing

The answer is 10, what is the question?

The answer is one moon, what is the question?

The answer is parallel, what is the question?

The answer is 365.25, what is the question?

The answer is conductor, what is the question?

Here are some temperatures taken from different cities around the world: London −4°, Moscow −6°, New York −9°, Paris +6°, Sydney +14°. What could the possible questions be?

Two particularly important strategies in both mathematical and scientific exploration are 'doing and undoing' and 'working backwards' and these types of questions also offer learners the opportunity to practise these skills. Most actions have a corresponding action; for example, we get dressed in the morning and undressed in the evening. It is the same with many mathematical and scientific ideas. With any doing, there is an associated undoing. This is helpful for learners to know. If, for example, they have solved a problem, they can now reverse that problem to begin to understand the process involved in solving it in the first place. With this approach, you can begin with simple questions and build up to more complicated ones.

Learners may begin by using a 'guess and check' strategy but soon they realise they can work backwards or undo the actions to discover what was 'done' to the number in the first place.

The next set of questions still start with the answer but, unlike the questions above, learners are looking for a specific answer to the question.

TEACHING ACTIVITY

Skills of reasoning: doing/undoing, working backwards, being logical

I am thinking of a number. When I add 3, the answer is 8. What is my number?

I am thinking of a number. When I subtract 7, the answer is 8. What is my number?

I am thinking of a number. When I multiply by 2, then subtract 2, the answer is 8. What is my number?

I am hard, cold, I melt when warmed. What am I?

I flower, have thorns and I have a fragrant smell. What am I?

I orbit Jupiter, my surface is icy, snow falls from my hot gasses. What am I?

---

8. How would you explain (justify) ...?

These types of questions demand more than a single answer or a simple description. They cannot be answered by providing a limited response and so by their very nature require at least an explanation, and probably a level of convincing and justifying; all characteristics we would recognise as **skills of reasoning**.

TEACHING ACTIVITY

Skills of reasoning: explaining, convincing, justifying, proving

How would you explain/justify:

Why the angles of a triangle add up to 180°?

Why an orange without peel sinks.

Why half of a half is less than a half?

Why a boat made of metal floats.

---

9. How many ...?

This is a very simple question that could almost be applied to anything. However, because the question is very open, it offers many possibilities – both in terms of the answer but also the approach learners could take in solving it. It is also a great question to ask learners to suggest a conjecture before they start solving it.

TEACHING ACTIVITY

Skills of reasoning: noticing, making connections, organising, explaining

How many triangles?

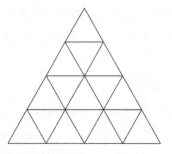

Figure 4.8 A triangle of triangles

Year 5 learners had a go at the question 'How many triangles?' Here are some of their responses.

The whole thing is a triangle.
Oh look! There's another one. It's got 4 small triangles.
See. There's more.
16.
No, there's more. There are triangles within triangles.
In every corner there is a triangle.

Using this question with an image enabled learners to draw on their knowledge of triangles without needing to directly ask them to describe or explain the properties of triangles. Instead, learners used their knowledge of triangles to begin to reason about how many there were, by first noticing some of the smaller triangles. However, the more they looked, the more they could see. All of the questions we have suggested in this chapter are more useful in enabling reasoning if learners are encouraged to work in pairs or small groups. The comments from the learners about triangles show how they bounce and feed off one another's noticings and observations.

How many rabbits?

A pair of rabbits has a litter of six.

Six rabbits find mates and have 26 young.

26 rabbits find mates and have 140 young.

How many rabbits?

How many males?

How many females?

10. Impossible questions

Using impossible questions challenges the notion that every question we ask has a correct answer. This is a particular assumption that learners often make with mathematics and science. However, one of the aims of this book is to support and extend learners' **skills of reasoning**, which can be problematic if they are continually seeking the right answer, rather than thinking about the concept or process. So, we suggest that it is useful to offer questions that are impossible to answer with just one number, word or phrase, in order to stimulate some rich explanations and perhaps some counter examples. These types of questions (and the way they are posed) appear to suggest a truth, that is of course not there!

Using impossible questions is also a great way to see if learners have any misconceptions. Misconceptions are inevitable, to be expected and yet are a great catalyst to effective learning. They open up the possibility for discussion and the chance to consider the understanding behind the misconception. Across mathematics and science, learners display many misconceptions, so rather than trying to avoid them or plan around them, why not pose questions that are themselves mis-conceptions about the two subjects? This will give learners the opportunity to begin to use their reasoning skills to either prove or disprove the misconception, as the questions above show.

11. Using 'See, Think, Wonder' as a way to ask questions

We offered this pedagogical approach as a type of scaffold to support reasoning in Chapter 2. It is particularly useful within this chapter as it centres on three different types of questions.

- See – what can you see?

- Think – what do you think is going on?

- Wonder – what does it make you wonder about?

The questions are asked in the order shown, which means that, at first, learners are simply say-ing what they see. Minimal thinking is occurring at this point. According to research by Harvard University (**www.pz.harvard.edu/projects/visible-thinking**) learners will often rush at a task and offer the first idea which comes to mind. By only allowing learners to say what they see, this technique encourages them to focus on the picture. The second question shifts the focus from not just saying what they see, but to encouraging learners to think about and make some hypoth-eses or conjectures about what might be happening. Finally, the third question begins to draw on curiosity and different **skills of reasoning** as it asks learners to go beyond the picture and con-sider other factors. This question encourages learners to be curious and pose questions, rather than just answer them.

──── TEACHING ACTIVITY ────

Skills of reasoning: noticing, describing, convincing, wondering

Choose a picture from the ones offered in Figure 4.9.

 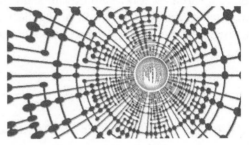

Figure 4.9 Four pictures to use with the 'See, Think, Wonder' scaffold

What do you see?

A big and small planet. Some colours and grey? They're circles … no … round.	A plant in the jungle. Leaves. Rolled up ones.
Hexagons. Three yellow ones in the middle.	A ship. A tunnel. Blue pattern.

What do you think?

They are really really big. An astronaut could go.	The flowers will be blue? It grows on the ground.
They could be a game. I like the way they fit together.	It goes forever? It's in space.

What do you wonder?

Is the small one small? Who lives there? How far away?	Does an animal live here? Does this grow round here? In the park?
Could we make these shapes? Would a pentagon fit?	Can I go there? Is it electric?

Using the 'See, Think, Wonder' framework is particularly useful in this chapter as the graduated questions probe different **skills of reasoning**. Even within the first question of 'What do you see?' learners are beginning to describe, which Pennant et al. (2014) would recognise as the first step towards reasoning (see Chapter 2 for more details on this). The 'What do you think?' question then begins to encourage learners to explain and perhaps even convince, the next stages of reasoning, according to Pennant et al. (2014). Finally the 'What do you wonder?' question allows learners to be creative, to connect ideas and to pose questions about what the picture has made them wonder about.

REFLECTION

Have you or your learners asked any thought-provoking questions lately?

Is there an odd number for every even number?

Can frogs live out of water?

Is there a 3D shape for every 2D shape?

Do monsters exist?

---

12. Using the question stems How? When? Why? Where? Who? What?

These six questions are typical questions we might use and hear in the primary classroom, in both mathematics and science lessons. They are often used to check understanding but can also prompt learners into thinking and reasoning, depending on the expectations of the answer. We often say that if teachers and learners used these questions more, particularly the 'Why?' question, learning would be better!

Here are some examples that we might hear in mathematics and science lessons. They could be about specific content or about how we work mathematically and scientifically.

Table 4.1 Examples of questions asked in mathematics and science lessons

Mathematical questions	Scientific questions
How many tens are there in 420?	**How** many planets are there?
When should we use the word 'product'?	**When** mould grows on food is it still safe to eat?
Why does an odd number added to another odd number always equal an even number?	**Why** do puddles dry up?
Where should I put this number on the number line?	**Where** does ice come from?
Who has the answer 10?	**Who** has the answer 'evergreen'?
What is the answer to 39 – 27?	**What** is your prediction for which material has least friction?

All six question stems could be used to ask an open or closed question. For example, *What* is the sum of 4 + 7? Or we could ask, *What* pairs of numbers can be added to give 11?

Although both questions use the 'What ... ?' question stem, the second question is more open because there are more possible answers. In both cases the question stem is useful, depending on what information the question requires. While the first question draws on a limited piece of knowledge, and requires recall of information, the second question demands more thinking and, as ideas are connected, **skills of reasoning** are used. As learners offer more examples for the second question, we can consider what the responses reveal about the understanding of combining two quantities together to total 11. For example, are the calculations offered organised in a systematic way? (e.g., 0 + 11, 1 + 10, 2 + 9, etc.); do they use both integer and decimal numbers? (e.g., 8.5 + 2.5, 6.1 + 4.9); do they employ negative numbers? (−3 + 14). Once learners begin to do something with their thoughts, perhaps organising them or connecting ideas, they have begun to move their thinking towards **reasoning**.

TEACHING ACTIVITY

Skills of reasoning: questioning, making connections, recognising links

Sometimes, these types of question stems can be used as a thinking frame for learners to organise their thoughts and pose questions about what it is they want to know.

Tell learners the next mathematics topic is on fractions. Ask them to pose questions that they would like to know about fractions, using the six question stems. For example:

How do we divide fractions?

When will I come across fractions?

Why do I need to use the same denominators when adding fractions together?

Where do fractions fit in our number system?

Who uses fractions in real life?

What is the numerator?

The next science topic is on plants. Ask learners to pose questions using the six question stems. For example:

How do plants grow?

When do they need water?

Why do they need oxygen?

Where is the best place to grow plants?

Who is the best person to look after plants?

What is the difference between a plant and a flower?

13. Using five more question stems: Does? Did? Can? Could? Might?

These question stems are very similar to those above, but can be used to draw on different **skills of reasoning.**

Mathematical questions	Scientific questions
Does two o'clock always follow after one o'clock?	Does sound travel faster than light?
Did the discovery of prime numbers contribute to our understanding of numbers and patterns?	Did the discovery of electricity help or hinder?
Can we be sure that 8 is an even number?	Can we change ice back to water?
Could you think of a shape that has two pairs of parallel sides and two right angles?	Could you describe what a journey into space could be like?
Might we think of a situation where zero has a value?	Might we be able to convince people not to use plastic bags anymore?

14. Using prompts as types of questions

A prompt is a statement, such as 'Tell me about ...', which has the same purpose as a question, as a response is expected. Just as we would intend when asking a question, a prompt can be designed to encourage some thinking, which would hopefully begin to connect ideas and move the thinking into using **skills of reasoning**. Like a question, a prompt is an invitation to do something, say something or suggest something.

— TEACHING ACTIVITY —

Skills of reasoning: generalising, explaining, comparing, describing

Tell me about the properties of quadrilaterals.

Tell me how evaporation occurs.

Tell me about this sequence:

Figure 4.10 A geometric pattern

Tell me about the lifecycle of a frog.

15. Questions from learners

Asking questions is the basis of mathematics and science. If mathematicians and scientists did not ask questions there would be little reason to reason! While any of the teaching activities and questions included in this chapter could just as easily be asked and explored by learners, the following sections look specifically at learners asking the questions, and not the adults.

As teachers, we model the skill of asking questions, but as we mentioned at the beginning of the chapter, teachers, but not learners, ask too many questions. If we want learners to work mathematically and scientifically (and we do) then being able to pose questions, as well as answer them, is essential and is also one of the **skills of reasoning**.

TRY THIS!

Create a space in the classroom where learners can pose and post their own questions. Encourage other learners to ask questions of the questions too.

Encouraging learners to think of the questions they would like to know more information about is often underrated, yet learners often ask the questions we haven't even thought about! At first this may seem daunting, but questions from learners should be celebrated and encouraged.

Consider these questions, all based on the topic of Space. At the beginning of the topic, the teacher asked the Year 2 learners what they would like to know. Here are some of their questions:

Why is the Sun in space?

Are there aliens in space?

Why is it so dark in space?

How does a rocket get into space?

How does the Earth compare to other planets?

Who could be out there?

What is Earth worth?

(6-year-olds)

These questions are all valid, because learners asked them. However, it also shows what they would like to know and find out about. As teachers we can sometimes think we know what learners are interested in, but we can also feel restricted by the curriculum we have to teach. However, the above questions can all be woven into the curriculum but starting from a point that learners are excited about.

Asking learners what they would like to know encourages creativity and begins to use **skills of reasoning** as they begin to connect ideas and organise their thoughts.

These questions also offer insight into what learners already know (and don't know), making these questions a useful assessment activity too. The following framework can provide a scaffold to enable this. It might be used at the beginning of a topic and then repeated at the end.

Table 4.2 Framework for questions to ask learners (KWL chart)

What do I already know?	What do I want to know?	What have I learned?

REASONING FOCUS

Do we value the questions learners ask enough?

Improving questions

Once learners have begun to ask questions, it is important to model how to improve a question. Show that you value all their questions; their question-asking is a key behaviour. Often learners will ask simple, straightforward questions to begin with. How fast does sound travel? What is the answer to 4 + 7? Providing some of the sentence stems and encouraging learners to use a variety of these can help them to begin to ask different types of questions; for example, How, Why, When, Might, Could, etc. Do not be afraid to ask learners if anyone can improve questions, beginning with your own. This shows learners that questions can have different roles and different purposes.

We also want to encourage learners to evaluate and refine their own questions and that of each other's. This is very common when developing a question for a science investigation. Learners need to notice that the way they use words has an effect on how the question is perceived, explored and answered. For example, asking:

Is a square a rectangle?

is not as powerful in inducing some of the **skills of reasoning** as

Are all quadrilaterals rectangles?

or

How can we stop the lolly melting?

is not as powerful in encouraging some of the **skills of reasoning** as

Which materials are the best thermal insulators?

REASONING FOCUS

Can we help learners 'improve' questions?

Do learners ask enough questions?

Would all learners' questions promote reasoning?

Can learners ask higher order questions?

Do learners have all the skills they need to pose powerful questions?

---

16. Learners asking questions to support them to critique their work and others

Several schools are now beginning to use what they call 'critique' as a tool to enable and support learners to be reflective about their learning. In its simplest form, critique is a way of offering kind words and praise to others for what has been achieved. A significant part of critique are the skills of noticing and questioning.

Critique provides feedback in a helpful and specific way, and using questions can promote thinking and reasoning about what it is that needs to be improved. Questions used effectively can halt children settling for first responses or drafts of work and support them in achieving far more than perhaps they realised. To begin with, the teacher may need to model the types of questions needed to support this process, but as learners gain understanding they can begin to take more control over supporting their peers. Many schools are using critique as part of their assessment for learning strategy.

Questions that we might encourage learners to use to critique their work and their peers are:

What would happen if ...?

Why don't you try ...?

Could you ...?

Have you thought of ...?

Have you considered ...?

What helped you to ...?

An example of learners asking each other questions to improve learning

Austin's Butterfly (**www.youtube.com/watch?v=hqh1MRWZjms**) is the story of a boy in the first grade (in Boise, Idaho) who had copied an illustration of a Western Tiger Swallowtail butterfly for his science project. However, Austin and his peers were learning the art of critique. While their rubric included traits of 'Being Helpful, Being Specific and Being Kind' when they gave feedback, they were ultimately tasked with providing Austin feedback on how to improve his first draft. They did this through asking a series of questions, related to the shape and details of the wings of the butterfly. Examples of the questions they asked included:

- How about the angle? (referring to the angle of the shape of the butterfly's wings)

- It's more like a triangle?

- Why don't you try adding some of the pattern?

In this example, questions are used in a different way and resulted in a remarkable six drafts for Austin to complete his masterpiece (the first draft is top left while the completed butterfly is bottom right)!

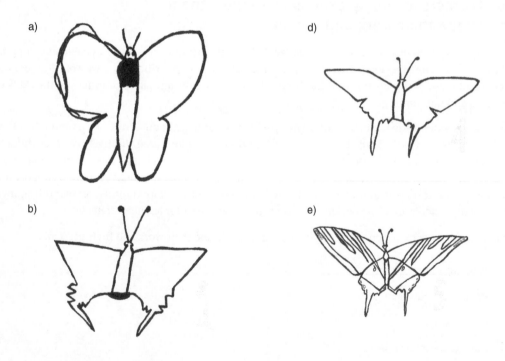

c)

f)

Figure 4.11 Student artwork by Austin. 'Austin's Butterfly.'

(Courtesy of ANSER Charter School in Boise, ID, part of the EL Education network. View online at Models of Excellence.
http://modelsofexcellence.eleducation.org/projects/austins-butterfly-drafts)

This approach may resonate with teachers who have recently (or not) adopted a 'mastery' approach to teaching. Mastery is not a new idea. Its origins can be traced to the early work of Benjamin Bloom (1968, 1971a, 1971b). However, perhaps a useful definition, and one that spans across both mathematics and science, is that from Carol Dweck (1986) who defined mastery as, *an approach in which learners seek to develop their competence by acquiring new skills and master new situations, with a focus on personal improvement and development.* The above example, from Austin, would seem to fit into this definition. Yet whether we consider this to be a form of mastery teaching or not, encouraging learners to ask questions of themselves and each other, as well as mathematical and scientific concepts, is another opportunity to draw on the **skills of reasoning**.

REASONING FOCUS

Can mathematics make me happy?

Is science more important than mathematics?

Can mathematics help you win?

Do you have to prove something to believe it?

What is the universe's favourite number?

CHAPTER SUMMARY

All forms of questions and questioning are useful. They are at the heart of both mathematics and science. But just as there are many **skills of reasoning** to draw on, there are also many reasons for questioning. The questions we have used in this chapter are designed to stimulate learners to

(Continued)

(Continued)

think and reason, as opposed to seeking one answer to a question. Often, the questions will generate another question and prompt learners into using some of the **skills of reasoning** we have identified in this book. In this way we are promoting questions to be a catalyst for dialogue, where learners exchange ideas and views, rather than try to find the answer the quickest.

However, the more learners can ask the questions, change the questions and improve the questions, the more it will help them to become better thinkers and reasoners.

Having read this chapter you will:

- know that all questions are useful;
- be clear about how questions in the classroom can lead to learners reasoning;
- have considered a wide range of different types of questions;
- have a developing toolkit of teaching approaches that all use questions to enable reasoning;
- know why questioning is one of the **skills of reasoning**.

5

USING PREDICTION, CONJECTURE AND HYPOTHESIS TO PROMOTE REASONING

IN THIS CHAPTER

By the end of this chapter you will:

- be clear about how prediction, conjecture and hypothesis assist learners to develop reasoning in science and mathematics;
- be clear about how prediction, conjecture and hypothesis by learners assists learning in both mathematics and science;
- have seen a number of examples of prediction, conjecture and hypothesis in science and mathematics which you could develop in your own classroom;
- know why prediction, conjecture and hypothesis are part of the **skills of reasoning**.

Introduction

This chapter will show that having learners use prediction, offer a conjecture or make a hypothesis is a very powerful vehicle for promoting thinking, and therefore reasoning, in both mathematics and science. Making assertions in the form of predictions, conjectures and hypotheses is useful in many parts of both mathematics and science and is strongly linked to problem-solving, pattern, value and relationships in both subjects. For example, astronomy uses pattern and mathematics to observe the night sky and predict the movement of objects; the movement of the planets has been studied and calibrated for hundreds of years, and is now very accurate. This means that very reliable predictions can be made. Other phenomena and conjectures about objects in space, such as black holes, are based on less evidence and so predictions become more speculative and hypotheses remain untested.

What are predictions, conjectures and hypotheses?

We might start by saying what they are not. None of these assertions are guesses. A guess is a speculation, an idea which may not be fully informed; it may be almost plucked from the air. Unlike a guess, predictions, conjectures or hypotheses are all linked to some form of logical, purposeful and goal-orientated thought, which we can recognise as a form of reasoning.

REASONING FOCUS

What confidence might we have in these statements?

- my guess is, next year I will get promoted;
- I guessed that she would be offered the leading role;
- I am sure these shares will rise in value;
- I think this winter will be very mild;
- she guessed the child's age to be nine or ten.

The examples offered in the Reasoning Focus above may be based on no information at all, or perhaps on a little. This is what makes each one a guess rather than something else. Last winter may have been mild or very cold but, without any other evidence, long-term weather forecasts based on little or no evidence are very challenging. Some guesses are just that, but we refer to others as an 'educated guess' – that is, they are based on some knowledge or experience. However, once we begin to make connections, employ evidence or notice patterns, for example, it becomes less of a guess and more of a prediction, conjecture or hypothesis.

A prediction, conjecture or hypothesis are all very similar in their purpose and it is often difficult to decide which term you are employing. While we offer definitions for each one below, our main purpose is to show how they all promote reasoning, rather than provide definitive definitions attached to each one.

Prediction

In mathematics and science, predictions are important as both subjects are about describing the world; where possible, quantifying the world so that reliable predictions, and even generalisations, can be made. If I need to feed my family, how many potatoes should I plant? What is the average yield of a potato plant? Which week is best to plant the seed potatoes? When can I expect a crop? All of the answers to these questions will be predictions based on previous growth of potatoes, weather and arithmetic. Predictions have perhaps been associated more with science than mathematics, although the purpose of making a prediction could easily be applied to mathematics too.

A prediction is a reasoned statement about what the predictor thinks will happen. It is reasoned because it is based on the predictor's knowledge and understanding of the phenomena, values or relationships in question, and is rational, purposeful and goal-orientated; for example, bubbles blown will be big or small (Figure 5.1). The fact that it is a statement is valuable in classrooms because, whether verbal or written, it evidences thought. This provides the teacher with an opportunity to enquire and question; for example, so why do you say that? The learner can explain and, with support, refine the prediction: *I think ... because ...* The statement gives the learner a baseline to then make a judgement about what is later observed or measured. It allows reflection and further reasoning; for example, My prediction was wrong so what have I learned? Do I need to think again about my understanding? I was right, is this going to work in other instances/is my understanding correct?

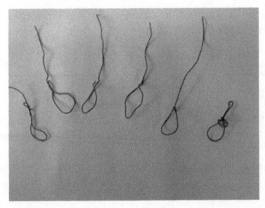

Figure 5.1 'We have made bubble blowers – we predict that they will make big bubbles' (5-year-olds)

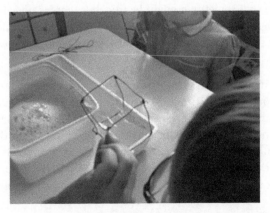

Figure 5.2 'I think this bubble blower will make square bubbles?' (6-year-old)

Weather forecasters would never, we suspect, describe their forecasts (predictions) as guesswork. Weather forecasting is a science called meteorology. It uses mathematical algorithms and masses of gathered and historical data to establish patterns and make predictions. Weather forecasters claim high levels of reliability in their predictions for short-term forecasts – for example, the next 6–12 hours – because they can see patterns and weather systems that they understand, and which usually behave in a predictable way. However, asked to predict a year in advance, meteorologists resort to long-term patterns about the climate where they can see broad trends; sadly they then have much less reliability about what will happen at a location in, say, early December a year from now, although they have moved a long way from weather being the result of anger or pleasure of the Gods! So much about the behaviour of the atmosphere is known that we now appreciate its complexity and chaotic nature, which in the longer-term makes it difficult to predict at the local level.

TRY THIS!

Ask your learners about situations when they make predictions - in games, when planning the day ahead, in lessons, and other times.

Ask colleagues in which subjects they ask learners to predict.

The example of weather forecasting assists us as we can perceive a continuum of reliability in predictions. Short-term weather predictions are based on very well-understood ideas and considerable amounts of reliable data. We can have a high degree of confidence in them. Other predictions are much less reliable, based perhaps on limited evidence or less well understood phenomena, so we would be sensible to limit our confidence in them.

Conjecture

A conjecture is very similar to a prediction but associated more with the world of mathematics. A conjecture is an assertion that something might be true, but there is no evidence yet known by the conjecturer to decide whether it is true or not. Conjectures are often (but not exclusively) linked to the search for pattern or structure. They too are logical, purposeful, and goal orientated and so, like predictions, fit within the skills we would recognise within reasoning.

A conjecture allows learners to pursue evidence and gather examples to test whether their conjecture is correct. For example, I might conjecture that 39 is a prime number because my experience of prime numbers (with the exception of 2) reveals that they are odd numbers and 39 is an odd number. One of the reasons for making conjectures is that they need to be checked out. This is the main purpose of making a conjecture and, as a result, it draws on many of the **skills of reasoning** we identified in Chapter 2. So, even though the conjecture about 39 being a prime number turns out to be wrong, we will have engaged in some useful mathematics in discovering why.

The conjecture about 39 being a prime number only involves one example. Other conjectures are much wider, and many have shaped much of our mathematical history as we currently know it. For example, Fermat's Last Theorem took 358 years to solve, and much effort from different mathematicians. Sometimes still referred to as Fermat's conjecture, Fermat's Last Theorem was finally proved in 1995 by Andrew Wiles (for more information watch the BBC short film where Andrew talks about his personal experience of seeking a proof, what it is like to do mathematics, to be creative, to have difficulties, to make mistakes but to persevere and succeed (**www.bbc.co.uk/iplayer/episode/ b0074rxx/horizon-19951996-fermats-last-theorem**). Many of the conjectures that learners will offer and test out in the classroom will have already been solved – but not by them.

It is interesting to note that the Latin roots of 'conjecture' mean to 'throw together'. In this sense we are throwing together many observations and evidence to form one idea. At this stage a conjecture is still an unproven claim. Once someone proves a conjecture it becomes a theorem. Pythagoras had a conjecture about right-angled triangles that was later proved, and which is now referred to as Pythagoras's Theorem.

So, unlike a prediction, a conjecture is a statement which appears to be true but has not yet been proven. While predictions also assume a certain truth, they are sometimes broader and not as focused on specific evidence as conjectures. For example, predicting that it might rain in the month of May might turn out to be true, but only be based on the fact that it has not rained for a month. While this is still better than a guess because it is using some evidence, it is not using previous data about the rainfall in May over the last couple of years, for example.

It is important to encourage learners to say what they think about what they notice, and then value their conjectures by writing them down, displaying them in the classroom, and testing them to see if they are true. Learners can then use their **skills of reasoning** to convince, justify, organise information, refute, disagree, or agree, for example. While it is important for learners to come up with their own conjectures, here are a few that you might want to offer as starting points for your learners.

- Look at the collection of containers and make a conjecture about which has the greatest capacity.

- $\frac{1}{2} + \frac{5}{7}$ is greater than 1.

- 12,404 is divisible by 4.

- All multiples of 6 are also multiples of 3.

- Multiplication always makes numbers bigger.

- All rectangles have exactly two lines of symmetry.

Some conjectures will only focus on specific cases (as with the example of 39 being considered a prime number). However, some conjectures extend into more general examples, as with the conjecture above, 'All multiples of 6 are also multiples of 3'. When the examples move into the general, this now becomes a generalisation. At this point the conjecture may be proved true or not, but it has now become an assertion that something is potentially true for a number of cases, or even in every case. A generalisation asks,

Will this always work or be true for any example? One of the hallmarks of mathematical thinking is the importance played by justification and generalisation; Chapter 8 explores this further.

TRY THIS!

Ask learners to offer conjectures about the mathematics they are working on. Do they notice a pattern that they can make a conjecture about?

Hypothesis

A hypothesis is a proposed explanation of a phenomenon (usually in science), and remains as such until proven by observational evidence. A hypothesis becomes a theory when it has been repeatedly tested so that it reliably explains and predicts what will happen. Such theories then allow us to make predictions from one instance to others. Often a hypothesis will emerge by noticing specific examples that are seen to have commonalities, so we can then speculate that this will always be the case. While a conjecture can be a hypothesis, a hypothesis tends to be a generalisation. Not all conjectures are generalisations; for example, '39 is a prime number'.

All three assertions (prediction, conjecture, hypothesis) relate to reasoned thought about what may happen, or explaining what happens. They all prompt a search for evidence to either prove or disprove. All three are significant in enabling learners to reason in mathematics and science. Without prediction, conjecture or hypothesis, how would learners be encouraged to question, notice, look for pattern and structure, explain, justify, and generalise? These three skills encourage learners to think about their thinking, and then to reason about what it is they think.

REASONING FOCUS

Mathematics looks for order; a sequence of numbers allows us to predict missing numbers. For example:

1, 2, 3, 4, 5 ...

2, 4, 6, 8, 10 ...

1, 1, 2, 3, 5, 8 ...

Without a perceivable pattern we can predict, but not confidently; this starts to feel like guesswork.

8, 17 ...

−4, +6 ...

However, is your guesswork educated by the way you have spotted patterns in the past? Can you make any conjectures?

Connecting mathematics and science through prediction, conjecture and hypothesis

Prediction, conjecture and hypothesis are all important in mathematics and science education because they require us to draw on things we know or observe, and ask us to think about other instances in the future. We are asked to make a reasoned statement about the future. They are all abstractions; a teacher's request for a prediction, conjecture or hypothesis may be one of the earliest requests for abstract thought. They are therefore educationally very valuable and key skills within reasoning.

Both mathematics and science are about observing and perceiving phenomena, values and patterns, so both subjects are interested in predictability which allows generalisation. Goldsworthy and Feasey (1997) gave four reasons towards the importance of prediction in science. We feel their model is particularly helpful, not just with prediction, but also with conjecture and hypothesis:

(1) prediction helps learners to think ahead and to make plans;

(2) it helps them focus on the key variables by asking them to anticipate the relationship between them;

(3) it gives them clues to the measurements that should be taken;

(4) giving reasons for predictions encourages them either to describe their everyday experiences from which they have made a generalisation or to explain the scientific knowledge on which they have based their predictions.

Prediction, conjecture and hypothesis move mathematics and science from a collection of observations and facts towards knowledge and understanding for action, including problem-solving. They all require learner engagement, they demand that we think about the future or a relationship and make an informed statement about what may happen. We would encourage you to ask learners to make predictions, conjectures and hypotheses as much as possible in both subjects. Try the examples in Table 5.1, stressing that to have value, predictions, conjectures and hypotheses don't always have to be right.

Table 5.1 Experience leading to prediction and conjecture and a following observation

What we know or have seen	Our prediction or conjecture	What transpires
Quadrilaterals have four sides and four right angles	This is true for all quadrilaterals	We found that a rhombus and other quadrilaterals don't have four right angles
The Moon appears to change shape and shrink	That it will shrink and then grow again	It does shrink but then appears to disappear

(Continued)

Table 5.1 (Continued)

What we know or have seen	Our prediction or conjecture	What transpires
As we move an object away from a light source its shadow gets smaller	This will continue and if we draw a graph we will see a straight line	The line of the graph is curved
In a classroom pots of warm water cool down	Our pot will cool down below 30 degrees centigrade	The water cools to room temperature
A woodlouse appears more active in bright light	The woodlouse will not move in near dark	The woodlouse is more active in the dark
Square numbers alternate odd and even in sequence	This will go on forever	We tested the first 30 square numbers and the pattern was true

The predictions offered in Table 5.1 enable learners to begin gathering evidence which could lead to changing their predictions and conjectures into generalisations. In Chapter 8 we explore further the importance of generalising within reasoning.

The skills of prediction, conjecture and hypothesis are all accessible forms of reasoning for young learners. It follows to and from observing and noticing, and links strongly to speculating, organising, questioning, generalising and more. Prediction, conjecture and hypothesis are important **skills of reasoning** for all primary-aged learners. As we outlined in Chapter 2, the **skills of reasoning** are not hierarchical and may be used in different ways at different times to suit the learner and the situation – as suggested by teachers in Figure 5.3.

A Web of Reasoning

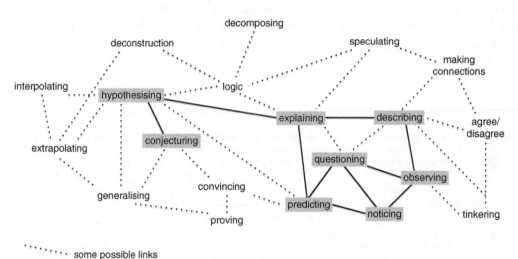

.... some possible links

- now draw in bolder lines to show the links you made & highlight the skills you used

A Web of Reasoning

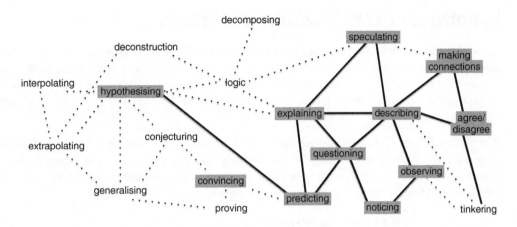

······ some possible links

- now draw in bolder lines to show the links you made & highlight the skills you used

*Figure 5.3 Teachers note that learners use different combinations of **skills of reasoning***

TRY THIS!

Ask your learners to make predictions and conjectures and to say how confident they are about them.

My prediction/conjecture	How confident I am and why
This ball dropped from 1m will bounce 22 cm high	Quite confident because: • when I dropped it from 25 cm it bounced 10 cm high • when I dropped it from 50 cm it bounced 14 cm • when I dropped it from 75 cm it bounced 18 cm
It will rain tomorrow	
The coin will land tails up	
I will roll a six on the dice	
The Sun will rise tomorrow	

You might add a third column on the right labelled 'What more information could I find to increase my confidence?'

Making prediction, conjecture and hypothesis explicit within the lesson

Prediction, conjecture and hypothesis have been recognised for years as important in primary mathematics and science education, but explanations about why this is so have not always linked directly to reasoning and thinking. In primary science, teachers often routinely ask for predictions but are perhaps not always clear about the enormous learning potential of predictions (Crossland, 2017). This is true also for conjectures in primary mathematics.

When a teacher asks learners to predict or offer a conjecture they are saying, look at this/these instance/s, think about it and make a reasoned statement about what might happen. They are requiring the learner to notice what is before them, notice features (mathematical and/or scientific) and speculate about related instances. Look at the Reasoning Focus below.

REASONING FOCUS

Height from which the ball is dropped	20 cm	40 cm	60 cm	80 cm	100 cm	120 cm
Height of the bounce	6 cm	8 cm	10 cm	12 cm	14 cm	... cm

Look at the data above and predict the next reading for a ball dropped from 120 cm. You could extrapolate from the data and reason that, based on the pattern, you can be confident that the bounce should be around 16 cm? We might also ask you to interpolate the bounce from 50 cm. Again, the pattern is useful but you have to take another step to suggest 11 cm. These are both predictions which may or may not be proved by testing.

Figure 5.4 Datalogging allows informed predictions based on recording measurements of temperature, light and sound

(www.data-harvest.co.uk)

Collecting data in the classroom can be very time consuming. Using Dataloggers (Figure 5.4) allows learners to see data very quickly, perceive patterns or anomalies and make reasoned predictions and conjectures about, for example, the next set of readings. Dataloggers are often found more frequently in the science classroom, yet they offer a wealth of data that would be just as useful in the mathematics classroom. Before learners get too excited about using the equipment, ask them to make a prediction, conjecture or hypothesis. Ask them why they think what it is they offer. Record their reasons and then let them go! A moment spent thinking, using the **skills of reasoning,** can strongly enable children's reasoned thought.

As mentioned earlier in this chapter, another important feature of prediction, conjecture and hypothesis is that they give us something to prove or refute. This consideration of evidence is at the heart of both mathematics and science. Our predictions, conjectures and hypotheses should be tested so that we can confidently say, that based on evidence to date, they represent our best understanding. This does not mean that we need to collect enough evidence to contribute to the mathematics or science body of knowledge that currently exists. Pursuing evidence is often more about the process of how we do this, rather than finding the answer. While learners are keen to reach an answer (often as quickly as possible), focusing on the skills we are using is already extending our knowledge base. In Figure 5.5 Year 4 learners begin their investigation on exploring friction by predicting and hypothesising which objects will travel the furthest. Including these two elements helps them to consider how to shape the experiment that will follow. We can also make use of these techniques, often found in science lessons, in mathematics learning.

REFLECTION

Young learners will often mistakenly assume that all predictions, conjectures and hypotheses have to be correct.

How would you encourage learners to realise that any prediction/conjecture/hypothesis is a good one?

All three skills are fundamentally linked to the notion of explanation, justification and thus to reasoning. To fully exploit these **skills of reasoning** teachers should add, And why? For example, We have seen the change in shadow size as we move the torch, what do we predict will happen when we move the torch even closer? And why does this happen? In mathematics it is similar; if we predict the outcome we must then seek an explanation. For example, if we increase the diameter of a circle by X, the area will increase by Z. Why is this? Predicting is often a useful prerequisite to conjecturing and hypothesising. While both conjectures and hypotheses attempt to state an irrefutable rule, law or generalisation, in mathematics these relationships can be established, and once proved they remain. In science, evidence is sought to prove or disprove the conjecture or hypothesis. Once evidence is found, the hypothesis becomes an established theory until conflicting evidence is discovered.

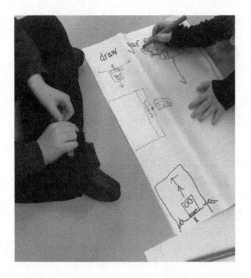 

Figure 5.5 Year 4 learners plan an investigation to test their hypothesis

Prediction, conjecture and hypothesis in investigations and problem-solving

Prediction, conjecture and hypothesis are each important in both mathematics and science investigations and problem-solving. As we have already said, in a science investigation it is always useful to make a prediction or test a hypothesis. In mathematics you might predict that given a problem, the answer is going to be in the range 1,000–2,000.

In Chapter 7 we offer a model for investigating and problem-solving from a mathematical perspective. In this chapter we consider investigating and problem-solving from a scientific one. As we echo continually throughout this book and elsewhere (Cross and Borthwick, 2016; Cross et al., 2016), one of the benefits in connecting these two STEM subjects together is the crossover they have. Whether we are problem-solving and investigating from a scientific or mathematical framework, both utilise and reinforce the **skills of reasoning** we are exploring.

Turner et al. (2011) refer to five types of investigation within a science context: observing over time; identifying and classifying; pattern seeking; secondary research; comparative and fair testing. Here we will consider: observing over time; pattern seeking; secondary research; and comparative and fair testing. While we explore these from a scientific perspective, notice how they could easily be within a mathematical one too.

Observing over time

Investigations in mathematics or science over time are ideal for predictions and conjectures: they invite prediction or conjecture. For example, These seeds have been sown, how do you predict that they will grow? What is your conjecture about their height? Speed of growth? A number of aspects of science require predictions over time; these are often in the biological or environmental areas we study. Consider these examples:

Table 5.2 Observations over time

Observation over time	Aspects of possible prediction often employing mathematics
Similar sized blocks of ice melting in different places in school	This one will melt first because ... All the blocks will melt within 24 hours because ... This one will make more liquid water than the others because ...
20 seeds of three different plants are sown	These seeds will grow tallest because ... Only $\frac{3}{4}$ of the seeds will germinate because ...
Plastic bags are tied over leaves to capture water vapour transpired from the leaf	We will collect 5 ml per day The leaf in the dark will not release water
Five steel nails are wetted for a week to encourage rust; four, however, have been treated to prevent rusting, one with BP jelly, one with oil, one with butter and one with paint	They will all rust but not the painted one because ... The untreated nail will be 100% rusty because ... The buttered nail will rust because ...

But we can take reasoning further here, in both mathematics and science. The prediction and an explanation for it make a huge contribution, especially if the prediction is framed in the language of the variables. For example, As I change the distance how will the size of the shadow change? Such conjectures may also lead learners to generalising. Whether the conjectures turn out to be proven or not, learners are thinking, reasoning, justifying, trying to convince their peers through evidence; all traits of thinking and working mathematically and scientifically.

Pattern seeking

Here questions lead to testing with specific objectives of identifying patterns and structure. Like other science investigation types, this links to mathematics. Chapter 6 explores the importance of noticing pattern and structure as a way of enabling the **skills of reasoning**.

Have a look at the questions below, which are designed to encourage learners to explore patterns and begin reasoning about the evidence they gather.

Q1 Do taller people have longer arms?

Q2 Does temperature affect the rate of growth of seedlings?

Q3 Do shadows get bigger when we move the light source away from an object?

Q4 When making ear defenders does every extra layer of sound insulation material halve the sound getting through?

As with other forms of investigation, each question invites a prediction or conjecture. The prediction should be articulated in a sentence so it is clear; for example, I think seedlings grow faster in warmer conditions. The value of the prediction is increased with the addition of explanation or justification; for example, I think seedlings grow faster in warmer conditions because cold can kill them. The requirement for an explanation strengthens the reasoning in the process. By encouraging, over time, explanations which employ more science knowledge, we move towards scientific generalisation; for example, I think seedlings grow faster in warmer conditions because things like photosynthesis slow down in the cold and speed up in warmer places.

Chapter 6 explores more examples of pattern seeking, including examples linked to mathematics.

Secondary research

All scientists and mathematicians conduct secondary research drawing on publications and electronic sources. Many (scientific) questions asked by learners cannot be answered practically or safely in the classroom. These are opportunities to search existing books, sources and data. Questions like these might be linked to prediction and conjecture.

Q1 How does day length vary during the year? Prediction – there is 15 minutes more light each day from January to June.

Q2 Do planets have more moons the further they are from the Sun? Prediction – planets close to the Sun don't have moons.

One valuable source of data are the annual mass involvement surveys – sometimes called citizen science – where people are asked to survey animals and plants in their locality and submit their findings. The 2017 UK Big Butterfly Count (Figure 5.6) saw 60,000 people submit 62,000 sets of data. From this Table 5.3 was produced (**http://bigbutterflycount.org/2017mainresults**).

A total of 73,161 Red Admiral butterflies were spotted, which is 75 per cent more than in 2016. Aside from the numerous questions which could be posed about this data, we could seek predictions and make conjectures. For example, how many Red Admiral butterflies might be seen by 60,000 people in 2018? Such predictions will vary, and that variation might be a very profitable focus of reasoned discussion about what influences butterfly numbers and how much deviation for error we might consider. Can you make any conjectures for 2018? 2020? 2030?

Data like this is real, up-to-date and based on a very large sample. This means that it is very valuable to us as teachers. It allows our learners to see real information, consider it, reason about it, pose their own questions and offer conjectures.

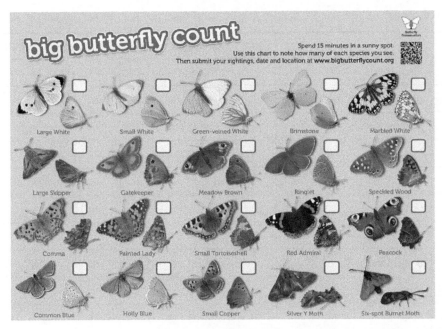

Figure 5.6 Free identification chart provided by the Big Butterfly Count

(http://bigbutterflycount.org)

Table 5.3 Results of the 2017 Big Butterfly Count

		Abundance	% change from 2016
1	Gatekeeper	93171	24%
2	Red Admiral	73161	75%
3	Meadow Brown	69528	−23%
4	Small White	61812	−37%
5	Large White	61064	−38%
6	Peacock	29454	1%
7	Comma	22436	90%
8	Small Tortoiseshell	20267	4%
9	Common Blue	19567	109%
10	Speckled Wood	18639	15%

(Continued)

Table 5.3 (Continued)

		Abundance	% change from 2016
11	Ringlet	18381	–57%
12	Green-veined White	16456	–38%
13	Six-spot Burnet	9517	–28%
14	Painted Lady	8737	31%
15	Large Skipper	6579	–49%
16	Holly Blue	5929	–5%
17	Small Copper	5814	62%
18	Brimstone	5281	–7%
19	Marbled White	4894	–67%
20	Silver Y	1923	–2%

(http://bigbutterflycount.org)

Other mass involvement surveys include:

Big Garden Birdwatch – **https://ww2.rspb.org.uk/get-involved/activities/birdwatch**

Big Seaweed Search – **www.nhm.ac.uk/take-part/citizen-science/big-seaweed-search.html**

Urban Tree Survey – **https://scistarter.com/project/349-Urban-Tree-Survey#sthash.zMRAVJ2A.dpbs**

The Big Bumblebee Discovery – **www.britishscienceassociation.org/the-big-bumblebee-discovery**

Treezilla – **http://treezilla.org**

British Geological Survey Email Earthquake Questionnaire – **http://earthquakes.bgs.ac.uk/questionnaire/EqQuestIntro.html**

UK Ladybird Survey – **www.ladybird-survey.org/recording.aspx**

Birdtrack – **https://app.bto.org**

National Insect Week – **www.nationalinsectweek.co.uk/events/welcome.html**

Comparative and fair testing

Simple tests that include comparison allow learners to consider what they know and have observed, then make a prediction or conjecture about what might happen. In primary education within an investigation we usually change one variable and observe or measure another. See this example:

Our question

When we vary the distance of a torch from an object, what is the effect on the size of the shadow formed?

Our prediction

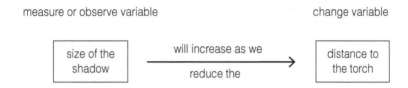

measure or observe variable   change variable

| size of the shadow | will increase as we ────────────→ reduce the | distance to the torch |

This format is one of several strengths of the 'sticky notes' method of planning and recording fair tests (Goldworthy and Feasy, 1997). This method links the selection of a measure (or observe) and change variable to the prediction. Thus learners are required to show that they have considered the testing to come, the variables and how they relate to one another (Figure 5.7).

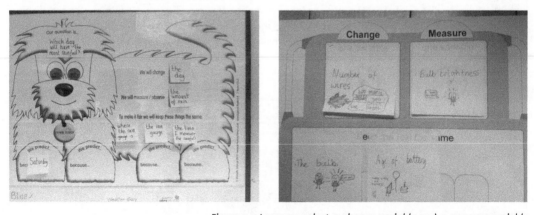

Figure 5.7 Learners select a change variable and a measure variable

The following section offers a range of activities that use prediction, conjecture and hypothesis, to draw on some of the **skills of reasoning**.

TEACHING ACTIVITY

Skills of reasoning: convincing, thinking logically, questioning, pattern seeking

Can your learners predict the likelihood of these events?

A footballer takes 100 penalties. Will she score 100 goals?

100 puppies run across a field, how many will find a bone?

100 children play in the mud, ten will come home clean.

You flip a coin 100 times, how many times will it land heads up and how many tails up?

You put new batteries in 100 clocks; when the batteries die none of the clocks stop at 12 o'clock.

TEACHING ACTIVITY

Skills of reasoning: observing, noticing, wondering, visualising, comparing

Place some coloured cubes in a bag. Ask learners to dip their hand into the bag and predict what colour they will pick out, but without looking. Once they have given their prediction ask them to check. Were they right? Repeat this process several times. Once lots of cubes have been seen, ask learners if they can predict with more accuracy. Have they noticed a pattern with the cubes? Can they offer any conjectures about the range of colours in the bag or the number of cubes that are red, blue or yellow, for example? What other pieces of information might help them to provide better predictions? (For example, the total number of cubes in the bag.)

Figure 5.8 Multilink cubes

TEACHING ACTIVITY

Skills of reasoning: noticing, pattern seeking, organising, observing, predicting, comparing, explaining

Figure 5.9 A shadow stick

Can your learners use a shadow stick (Figure 5.9) to observe how its shadow moves and changes in length over a day? They might record on paper and/or chalk on the floor to record the position and length of the shadow. On each occasion ask them to predict what will happen next, or during the day, and why?

You might illustrate this by taking readings and completing a chart on **www.childrensuniversity. manchester.ac.uk/learning-activities/science/the-earth-and-beyond/shadows**.

TEACHING ACTIVITY

Skills of reasoning: pattern seeking, being logical, describing, observing, verifying

Exploring patterns in any mathematical or scientific context are ideal activities to invite learners to make conjectures about what comes next. Have a look at this number pattern.

134, 234, 334, 434 ...

Can learners offer a conjecture about the next number? The 10th number? The 100th number? Can they offer a generalisation about the number pattern?

TEACHING ACTIVITY

Skills of reasoning: observing, comparing, noticing, organising, tinkering

Can your learners predict which gloves will feel softest? Keep their hands warmest? Keep a sealed pot of water warm for longest? Can they justify their prediction? Can they talk about the features of materials which stop heat moving? (Figure 5.10)

Figure 5.10 Gloves made from different materials

You might them ask them to devise a test to see which material is the best for stopping the heat moving from a hot material to a colder material.

TEACHING ACTIVITY

Skills of reasoning: noticing, comparing, describing, explaining

Ask your learners to throw a die 60 times but first predict how many times each number will come up. For example:

Number on die	I predict this number
1	12 times
2	4 times
3	13 times
4	8 times
5	8 times
6	15 times

Remember to ask learners to explain their predictions.

TEACHING ACTIVITY

Skills of reasoning: observing, explaining, predicting, noticing, predicting, describing, extrapolating, notice, pattern spotting, justifying, speculating

Can your learners look at a tally chart, pictogram or graph like the one in Figure 5.10, describe it, say what it says but then use it to make a prediction? For example, this graph tells us about the fruit eaten by a class of 35 children on one summer's day. If we were starting a school fruit shop at playtime, what would you order to sell over one week?

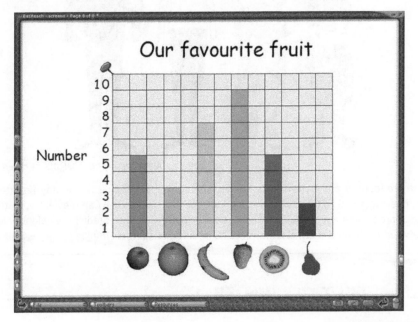

Figure 5.11 Bar graph

TEACHING ACTIVITY

Skills of reasoning: observing, explaining, predicting, noticing, extrapolating, pattern spotting

Can your learners select children from different age ranges throughout the school? After arranging them in order of age can they identify features which may change in a predictable way, e.g., height, arm span, hand span, foot length, mass, circumference of the head?

Figure 5.12 A human graph – heights at different ages

Can learners identify any patterns? Is there a correlation between age and any features? Can learners interrogate this data - for example, might there be any error? Can they extrapolate to use the data to predict the age of older learners? Can they interpolate to predict the height of learners aged between those measured, e.g., 7.5 years? Can they explain their thinking?

CHAPTER SUMMARY

Mathematics, and to a lesser extent science, are commonly thought to be subjects concerned only with finding right or wrong answers. While there are aspects within both subjects that do focus on finding the answers to questions or problems, this is only a very small part of learning mathematics or science. The most important, and largest, part of these two subjects is the ability to think and explore. Prediction, conjecture and hypothesis allow us to consider the different possibilities to situations and to view things in different ways. Their very nature encourages us not to focus solely on the answer, but to explore and ask questions. Supporting learners to adopt a predicting attitude or creating an atmosphere of conjecturing and hypothesising encourages the mathematical and scientific thinking and reasoning that we have been exploring in this book.

Having read this chapter you will:

- be clear about how prediction, conjecture and hypothesis assist learners to develop reasoning in mathematics and science;
- be clear about how prediction, conjecture and hypothesis by learners assists learning in both mathematics and science;
- have seen a number of examples of prediction, conjecture and hypothesis in mathematics and science which you could develop in your own classroom;
- know why prediction, conjecture and hypothesis are part of the **skills of reasoning.**

6

NOTICING PATTERN TO PROMOTE REASONING

——— IN THIS CHAPTER ———

By the end of this chapter you will:

- understand how noticing pattern and pattern spotting are both opportunities for learners to reason;
- explore the different forms pattern can take;
- explore how data provides a rich source for noticing patterns;
- have some activities to trial which encourage learners to notice patterns;
- know why noticing pattern and pattern spotting are **skills of reasoning**.

Why is noticing pattern important in enabling reasoning?

Pattern is all around us. We can see patterns in numbers, in data, in flowers and even within our own fingerprints. Humans are so tuned to notice pattern that they will often 'see' it even when it does not exist; in clouds, for example. That said, our ability to perceive patterns helps us enormously. Recent research has even suggested that young learners' ability to notice patterns can predict later mathematical achievement (Rittle-Johnson et al., 2016).

Patterns suggest order; they give us the gift of predictability (see Chapter 5). Pattern is therefore very important in both mathematics and science (Cross and Borthwick, 2016) and is a huge enabler of reasoning. However, pattern (like many of the other **skills of reasoning**) draws on other skills, too. For example, if a learner has noticed a pattern, they might begin to describe it, explain it, wonder about it. They may decide to correct it (if they perceive it is wrong), begin to ask questions about it, convince someone else about its structure or predict what will come next or what went before. They may also start to offer generalisations about it, which, as Chapter 8 notes, might encourage learners to begin gathering more evidence to begin proving or disproving the pattern; one of the hallmarks of being a mathematician or scientist. Blanton et al. (2015) suggest that pattern is important in developing early algebraic thinking, because patterns are often about the relationships between objects or features. Noticing similarities and identifying relationships between phenomena allows us to investigate whether these are regularities that might cause us to ask, Will this always work?

Being able to notice and spot pattern is an important skill in its own right, but it is also essential for identifying other relationships in mathematics and science, such as counting and understanding number operations, as the examples in Figures 6.1, 6.2 and 6.3 show.

REFLECTION

What is meant by the term 'pattern'?

What do you mean by the term pattern? Do you think of repeated symbols? What about a dress pattern?

What is a pattern?

By pattern we should distinguish between objects or symbols arranged or appearing in a way which is ordered or follows a rule (for example, see the number patterns below and the patterns of the faces in Figure 6.1), and a pattern which is a model to be copied (Tapson, 1996).

0.1   1   10   100   1000

Figure 6.1 Two examples of a pattern which is following a rule

By this latter definition, a pattern may be something that is to serve as a model to be copied; for example, a pattern in a motif such as the outline of an apple motif used by a computer manufacturer (Figure 6.2). Repetition, in some way, underlies all patterns. However, this repetition can manifest itself in many ways.

Figure 6.2 An example of a motif that can be copied

Which of these would you see as:

(a) a model which might be copied?

(b) one which manifests order or a rule?

- o   the Fibonacci sequence

- o   an audience performing a Mexican wave

- o   Morse code

- o   the constellation Orion

Could your learners identify pattern in:

•   a Morse code distress call?

•   computer coding?

•   a sunflower?

•   multiples of six?

Can learners see pattern in the natural world? In these pictures?

  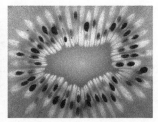

Figure 6.3 Examples of real life images which contain patterns

One of the **skills of reasoning** is to ask, Is what I see following an order or a rule? Some patterns can be harder to see; for example, dunes in a desert. Perhaps it depends on your viewpoint? A small insect in the desert might not perceive the pattern, but fly over the desert at 3,000 metres and the pattern, once unnoticed, is plain to see.

TRY THIS!

Ask learners and teachers to give you an example of a pattern.

Do they all default to a repeating pattern first?

Another important element when noticing pattern is to identify the unit of repeat. This enables learners to see a group of objects as one item (this is also key when moving learners from additive to multiplicative reasoning). Recognising the unit of repeat also focuses on the part–whole relationship of the objects or phenomena, which in turn supports learners' understanding of composition of numbers and other mathematical or scientific elements. Units of repeat can also be the basis for learners identifying the rules or structures in the pattern or structure. This helps learners to go beyond the simple repeating AB pattern and notice more complex units of repeat.

As learners begin to notice and develop pattern awareness, it may be that they recognise only one or two elements to begin with. For many, it is simply how they first noticed the pattern (for example, the pattern in colour, shape, size, etc.). They may need some further support to notice further elements.

Connecting mathematics and science through noticing pattern

We have already said that we believe pattern is all around us (Cross and Borthwick, 2016). Mathematicians study and search for patterns in numbers, geometry and data, while scientists look for patterns to make phenomena predictable. Noticing pattern is an opportunity to observe, predict, hypothesise, explore, discover and create. In both mathematics and science, pattern allows rules to be established (and broken) and without pattern both subjects would lack structure or clarification. While pattern pervades both mathematics and science, researchers in both disciplines have their own views as to how pattern can be described and defined.

Papic et al. (2011) suggest three types of pattern in mathematics:

- shapes with regular features, such as having equal sides and angles;

- a repeated sequence, such as red, blue, green; or ABAB or ABBA;

- a growing pattern, such as a staircase with equal steps.

Papic et al. suggest that learners who can notice patterns are usually able to repeat the pattern and predict how it might continue. This is a very important skill in science as we can never test every instance; for example, the bounce of every ball. Rather, we test a sample and extrapolate from that.

How does pattern help learners to think and reason?

In Chapter 2 we identified possible **skills of reasoning**, which included pattern seeking, although we would also use phrases such as pattern awareness, pattern spotting and noticing pattern interchangeably here, too.

Often learners may be able to solve a calculation, such as 6 × 4, but not understand the laws and structures around multiplication. Noticing the possible patterns in the numerical structure below might help learners solve the calculation in a different way.

Do learners see 6 × 4 as:

6 + 6 + 6 + 6

or

4 + 4 + 4 + 4 + 4 +4

or

....

or

(6 × 2) + (6 × 2)?

Perhaps this is the difference between teaching learners about multiplication or teaching them how to multiply? Is it that some learners do not stop to notice the things they are doing, or that some learners do not have pattern awareness? If learners were to notice patterns within mathematical and scientific structures and to reason about them, they might realise that they know a lot more than they think.

One element of reasoning is that you notice when you do not need to calculate. Pattern spotting can help you with this.

1 × 9 = 9

2 × 9 = 18

3 × 9 = 27

4 × 9 = 36

5 × 9 = 45

What patterns do you see? As a teacher you will know about the sum of the digits in the product of multiplying multiples of nine together as always adding to nine. Can you use the pattern to calculate 20×9, 35×9, $n \times 9$?

Similarly, we can use $3 + 5 = 8$ to help us to notice the relationship in $3 + 15 = 18$ and then in $3 + 25 = 28$. Noticing these types of patterns has significant bonuses as they lead to shortcuts in calculating!

Patterns in science are often obvious – for example, in the growth of a seedling – but at other times not so much; for example, all metals are magnetic (are they?).

TRY THIS!

In your maths and science lessons, make pattern seeking a medium-term objective. Can pattern be identified in lessons about: fractions? plants? Earth in space? shape? multiples of numbers? and more?

The importance of data in pattern spotting

Mathematics and science both use data to solve problems and investigate. The first step is to recognise that an event or value can be represented by something else. Then we can move to reading and interpreting the data and later manipulating data. Data provides a rich source to begin to notice pattern and then to re-create it.

REASONING FOCUS

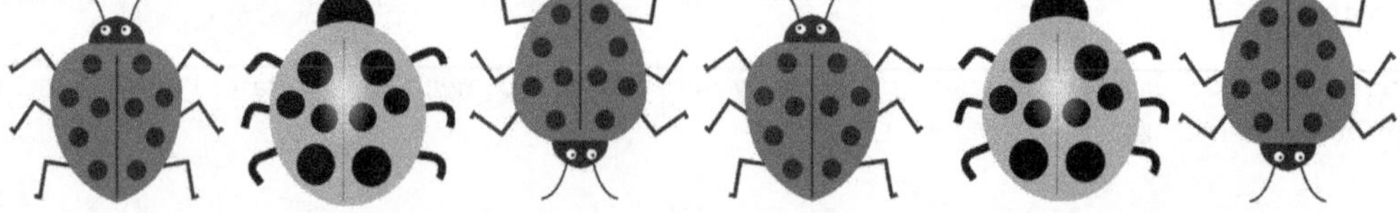

Figure 6.4 Look at the ladybirds – what patterns can you see?

Very young learners will love repeating patterns in sound, objects, motifs, movement, colour and shapes. In music or mathematics we can make patterns in drum beats and ask that they continue the pattern. We might ask them about patterns on clothing or in art: Can they see the pattern? Talk about it? Continue it? Can they invent their own pattern? Looking for pattern in the world around us is a very natural thing for humans to do. When observing Figure 6.4, which pattern did you see first? Did you then spot others? Did you adopt a strategy? Counting? Recalling previous situations? Say out loud?

Did you think about how the sequence might continue?

Having discussed examples of pattern in the world, the following section deals specifically with data, a very rich area for reasoning.

Reasoning through recording data physically

Initially, and at times, learners will record results in a physical way which closely resembles the occurrence or value; for example, with string or chalk.

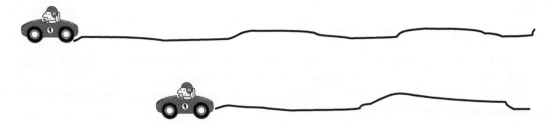

Figure 6.5 An example of recording results in a physical way

Can they reason that the chalk line is a record of what happened? Can they explain why one line is longer than the other? Can they predict the result of a third trial? Can they give a reason for their prediction? They might count floor tiles or carpet squares.

On other occasions, young learners will count or place coloured beads in jars; for example, every time a paper dart hits a target they put a red bead in a pot. If this is recorded with interlocking cubes they can be joined to form strips. Different strips can then be compared (Figure 6.6).

Figure 6.6 Interlocking cubes

Can learners recognise the collection or strip of cubes as a record of what happened? Can they say what will happen next? Or if we repeated it again? Or what would happen if we changed something? Can they consider possible outcomes? Reason about them?

Reasoning through recording data using tally charts

Tally charts present another opportunity to represent data. Initially, each mark represents one, but that can change later on.

	Monday	Tuesday	Wednesday
birds	❘	ⵆⵆ	❘❘❘

Even simple tally charts provide opportunity to pattern spot and reason. Is there a reason that we saw more birds on Tuesday? Can we make a conjecture?

Recording data using pictograms

Similar to tables are pictograms, which communicate a lot to young learners in a very accessible way. Young learners can make 3D pictograms; for example, they can stand in a line tallest to shortest and become a human graph. Another popular task is to ask learners to observe a puddle evaporating using marked Wellingtons to show the depth of the water reducing day-by-day. After several days the Wellingtons are displayed as a visual record/3D graph of the events. Can learners say what they see? Can they see a pattern? Would that pattern continue?

In a pictogram, children learn that a symbol can stand for an occurrence. They also learn about values on scales, and that symbols can be given a range of values.

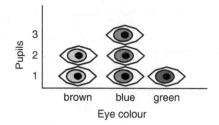

Recording data using block graphs

Similar to pictograms, now each occurrence is represented by a block, with categorical and discrete data labelled on scales, axes labelled, and tables and charts given titles. Block graphs can be orientated vertically or horizontally.

Learners may be asked to draw these on squared paper and on a computer.

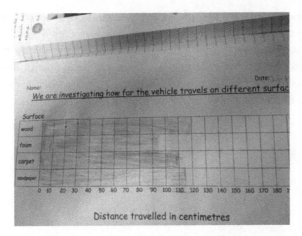

Figure 6.7 7-year-olds investigate friction

Reasoning through recording data using bar charts

These are similar to block graphs but employ different blocks to represent quantities.

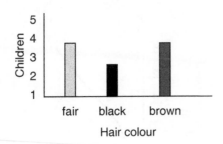

Figure 6.8 Chart to show hair colour

The data remains categoric or discrete: you can't have half a child or half a fair hair.

Recording data using line graphs

Here, the blocks are replaced by single lines.

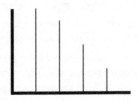

Figure 6.9 An example of a line graph

Graphs become very useful when we join points to create a line. This works when we have continuous data. Our readings are plotted, and the line drawn. Based on these readings we can be confident that readings we might make between the values would have results on this line. We are reasoning about new values based on a limited number of readings. We could take an infinite number of readings for rolling a ball down a ramp 3.1 cm high, 3.11 cm high. Unless there is a reason, there is no need to make so many measurements when we are confident in a pattern.

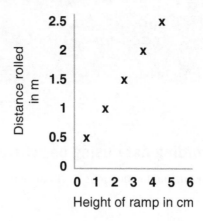

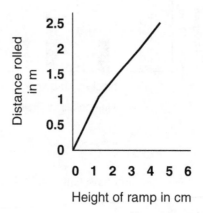

Figure 6.10 Results of tests rolling a ball down different ramps

Sets of data in whatever format offer us multiple opportunities to pursue the **skills of reasoning**, but in particular, pattern seeking. Graphs are familiar to us as we are used to teaching about: the graph's title, its axis, scale, marking/reading points; to order readings; to select the scale on the graph; and to join points. Once these skills are mastered do we then go on to explore the potential of graphs for reasoning and pattern spotting? Ought we to: see, identify and consider anomalous readings? draw a line of best fit?; interpolate?; extrapolate? Should we consider: any questions we had or predictions we made?; hypotheses we postulated?; new questions?; new sets of data we might seek?

REASONING FOCUS

Telling the story of the graph

Teachers will be familiar with the fact that tables and graphs tell a story; a story of values chang-ing in relation to one another. The graph in Figure 6.11 tells the story of a child's journey to school. Does this ask for reasoning? Why is the line flat here? Steep here?

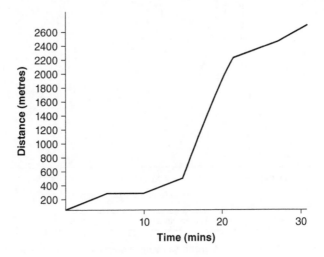

Figure 6.11 Graph showing the journey of a learner travelling to school

Can you explain what was happening at points a–e?

What was the fastest part of the journey? Why might that be?

What was the slowest part of the journey? Why was that so?

What would the graph look like if it had all been by car? By plane? 30 minutes longer?

Could you devise further questions which others might be tasked to answer?

Valuable learning can come from learners looking at possible graph shapes and predicting which might suit a scenario. If a room is warmed with a heater then what shape would a graph of the temperature be?

Look at Figure 6.12. Can you answer these questions?

- Why do the lines fluctuate so much?

- Why do the curves for the bold and fine lines differ?

- What is the trend over the seven days?

Primary teachers can invent data in order to construct graphs. We would argue, however, that it is best to use real or simulated data linked to the real world; ideally real data is best gathered and

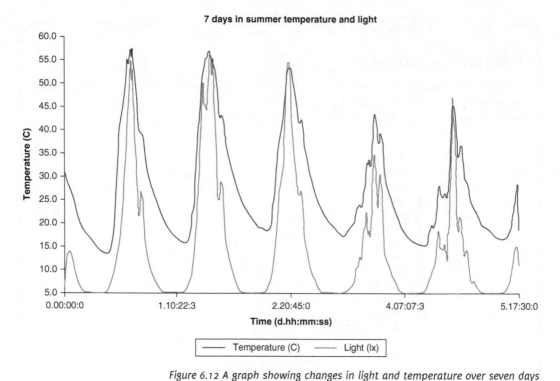

Figure 6.12 A graph showing changes in light and temperature over seven days

(Graph reproduced with permission from Data Harvest Group)

interpreted by learners. But there are limits to the amount of data a class can gather in a weekly science lesson or even a daily mathematics lesson. Numerous interactive simulations exist where websites can provide simulations, such as this one:

www.shodor.org/interactivate/activities/RabbitsAndWolves

Learners can input the number of rabbits and wolves in a habitat, set the simulation running and pause it to see a graph showing how the population sizes of grass plants, rabbits and wolves change over time. This particular simulation produces line graphs where relative population sizes can be observed as they fluctuate within the simulation. This simulation illustrates how populations of producers (grass), prey (rabbits) and predators (wolves) interact. The patterns in the population graphs influence one another.

As a teacher, can you see how this would help us teach about food chains? Food webs? Evolution? Evolution is all about what happens to populations of animals in future generations. What would happen if some rabbits were born that could run faster than wolves? Or if some wolves were born with very good camouflage? This is a good example because there is range of potential outcomes which is a feature of complex systems. Much about things occurring in the real world is the interaction of different factors. Reasoning helps us weigh these up and consider different outcomes. Like chess, for example, it enables our brains to examine multiple possibilities.

Pattern in nature

Patterns occur in nature for all sorts of reasons. The ripples of sand on a beach are affected by the angle of the beach, the speed of moving seawater, grain size and rock type. Other patterns occur in animal behaviour, populations and in features such as camouflage. A herd of running zebra makes a stunning spectacle but to a chasing predator, it is a confusing sight. So do zebra stripes mean there is safety in numbers? Safety in pattern? Can learners reason about this? About changes in the pattern? Or in herd-related habits? About predator eyesight? Or hunting techniques? Was there a time in the past when zebra were not striped or had different stripes? Did some stripe patterns afford more protection than others? Would this mean that zebra with less effective patterns would be caught and killed, allowing those with better stripes to survive and breed? Is this an example of Evolution by Natural Selection? (Darwin, 1859).

Figure 6.13 Camouflaged skin assists who? Predator or prey?

The following section offers a range of activities that use pattern, to enable and encourage learners to reason.

TEACHING ACTIVITY

Skills of reasoning: observing, organising, comparing, decomposing, pattern seeking, extrapolating, interpolating

When is a pattern a pattern? We are all aware of repeating patterns which follow a rule; for example, on wallpaper. But pattern can mean a motif, which may be repeated. The pictures below

(Continued)

(Continued)

(Figure 6.14) all demonstrate some kind of order of a pattern being followed. Ask learners to describe the pattern. Can they explain it?

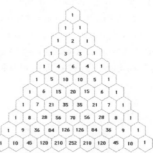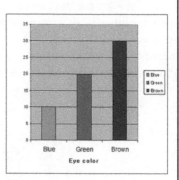

Figure 6.14 Different examples of pattern

TEACHING ACTIVITY

Skills of reasoning: observing, proving, justifying, altering, systematic doing/ undoing, tinkering, describing, agreeing/disagreeing, altering

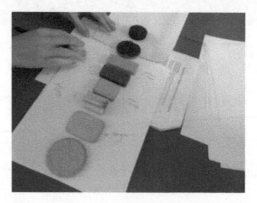

Figure 6.15 Pattern spotting in the evolution of biscuits

Can learners reason about possible evolutionary patterns in sets of sweets or biscuits? Ask them to examine a selection of biscuits or sweets and then, working in a group, to place the biscuits from more simple to most complex, in an order which models evolution. Then ask learners to explain and justify the order they determined.

TEACHING ACTIVITY

Skills of reasoning: noticing, visualising, being logical, making connections

Give learners lots of opportunities to copy patterns. This is not as easy as it sounds. Here are a few examples.

Build a tower of interlocking cubes using two/three/four colours. Ask learners to copy the pattern exactly to make an identical tower.

Place objects in a line. For example, shell, stone, shell, stone. Can learners copy the pattern with the same objects? What if you change the objects but ask them to copy the pattern?

Show learners a picture. Can they copy the picture? Remember this is not a memory test, so they are able to see the picture at all times!

TEACHING ACTIVITY

Skills of reasoning: noticing, pattern spotting, describing, questioning

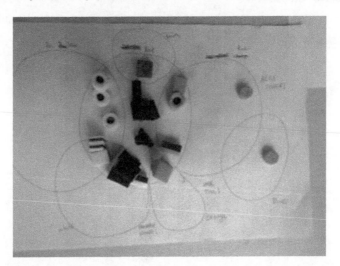

Figure 6.16 Grouping sweets

Can your learners group everyday objects like 3D shapes, rocks, 2D shapes, sweets, etc.? Encourage them to find other ways to organise sets of toys, books, leaves and more. Encourage them to look in more and more detail at objects so that they can identify difference, similarity and groups sharing features. Can they discuss and reason about different possibilities? Is one grouping more logical than another? Do they spot any patterns?

TEACHING ACTIVITY

Skills of reasoning: noticing, describing, explaining, extrapolating

Give learners numerical patterns. Ask them to notice the pattern, describe it and then extend it.

1, 2, 3, 4, 5 ...

2, 4, 6 ...

1, 2, 3, 5, 7 ...

Ask them, What is the next term? (next number). What about the 10th term? The nth term?

TEACHING ACTIVITY

Skills of reasoning: deconstructing, observing, classifying, making connections

Remember that some patterns do not always follow a linear structure. Look at the image in Figure 6.17. Can learners spot any patterns?

Figure 6.17 What patterns do you notice?

TEACHING ACTIVITY

Skills of reasoning: noticing, refuting, correcting, comparing, explaining, justifying

Give learners examples where the pattern is incorrect. Can they correct the error?

1, 3, 5, 6, 9

88, 77, 68, 58

red, blue, blue, red, blue, red, red

Perhaps in the last example, the pattern is correct, but it just appears incorrect because we have not yet seen the unit of repeat. Discuss this with learners. What do they think? Can they reason that it is correct or incorrect? What evidence do they use to convince and justify their reasoning?

TEACHING ACTIVITY

Skills of reasoning: observing, wondering, predicting, verifying

Predicting pattern is fun! Give learners a calculator, ask them to key in 2 + + and then notice what happens to the answers. Can they spot the pattern? Where will it end? Can they predict a number that will appear in this pattern?

Figure 6.18 A calculator

(Picture from Pixabay)

TEACHING ACTIVITY

Skills of reasoning: deconstructing, explaining, being systematic, comparing

Patterns are everywhere, even in children's literature. Read the story *One Is a Snail, Ten Is a Crab*. While this is a counting story, there is a developing pattern as to how the next number is created. Ask learners to predict what it could be.

Figure 6.19 One Is a Snail, Ten Is a Crab

This book is also available on **www.slideshare.net.** This is a free online service that hosts many slides that can be shared electronically in the classroom.

TEACHING ACTIVITY

Skills of reasoning: deconstructing, explaining, being systematic, comparing

This is an example of a growing pattern, but at each step more dots than in the previous step are added. Can learners explain the pattern? Can they extend it?

Figure 6.20 A growing pattern of dots

TEACHING ACTIVITY

Skills of reasoning

Ask learners to make up their own patterns. How complicated do they make them? How many different pattern elements do they include? What is their unit of repeat?

Once learners have created their own patterns, ask their peers to notice, describe, explain and extend the pattern.

CHAPTER SUMMARY

This chapter has explored the importance of noticing pattern as a way of enabling reasoning with learners. As with all the **skills of reasoning** that we are exploring in this book, each individual skill contributes to the development of mathematics and science in its own right. However, when we consider these skills, in this case, noticing pattern, we are able to see how important they are in developing the role of thinking and reasoning with learners.

Having read this chapter you will:

- understand how noticing pattern and pattern spotting are both opportunities for learners to reason;
- be able to explore the different forms pattern can take;
- be able to explore how data provides a rich source for noticing patterns;
- have some activities to try out that encourage learners to notice patterns;
- know why noticing pattern and pattern spotting are **skills of reasoning**.

7
USING PROBLEM-SOLVING AND INVESTIGATION TO PROMOTE REASONING

──── IN THIS CHAPTER ────

By the end of this chapter you will:

- understand the place of problem-posing, problem-solving and investigation within reasoning;
- know how different types of problems and investigations offer different opportunities for reasoning;
- understand that pupil autonomy when investigating and solving problems has the potential to enhance opportunities for reasoning;
- have a bank of activities to use within a problem-solving and investigation context that enables learners to use their reasoning skills;
- know how problem-solving and investigation contributes to the **skills of reasoning**.

How do problem-solving and investigation connect to reasoning?

At the heart of both mathematics and science education are problem-solving and investigation. To be successful in both mathematics and science, learners need to construct their understanding through solving problems and investigating. Both occur in mathematics and science and both are very important in mathematics and science education. Neither problem-solving nor investigation is unique to mathematics or science, but one might struggle to conceive of mathematicians or scientists who do not engage in these activities. These activities push the boundaries of understanding and lead us to reason. They allow us to solve non-routine problems that are neither predictable nor familiar. The **skills of reasoning** that we draw on will help us to deal with daily life but also solve the problems of the future.

Problem-solving and investigation require a range of skills, including those of reasoning. To understand the place and purpose of reasoning within problem-solving and investigation the model offered by Kilpatrick et al. (2001) is particularly helpful. While this model is often associated with a mathematical context, the connections between mathematics and science are so strong that this model also assists our understanding for science problems and investigations.

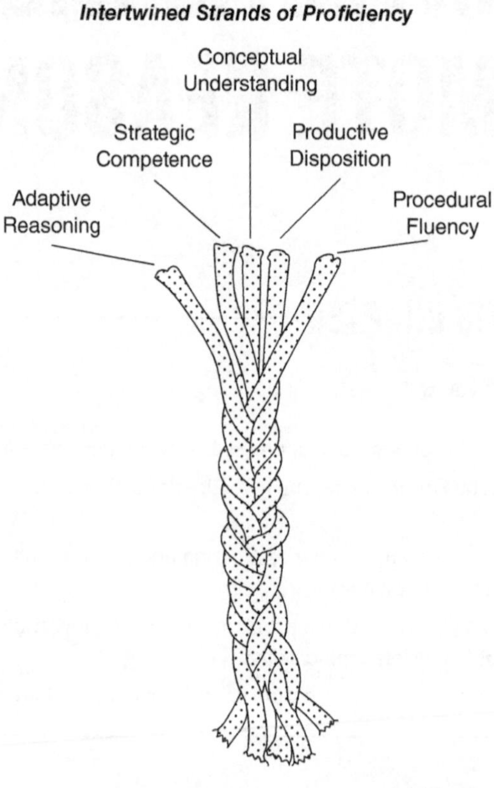

Intertwined Strands of Proficiency

Conceptual
Understanding

Strategic
Competence

Productive
Disposition

Adaptive
Reasoning

Procedural
Fluency

Figure 7.1 Five strands of proficiency

(Kilpatrick et al., 2001)

Adaptive Reasoning – capacity for logical thought, reflection, explanation and justification.

Strategic Competence – ability to formulate, represent, and solve mathematical [and scientific] problems.

Conceptual Understanding – comprehension of mathematical [and scientific] concepts, operations and relations.

Productive Disposition – habitual inclination to see mathematics [and science] as sensible, useful and worthwhile, coupled with a belief in diligence and one's own efficacy.

Procedural Fluency – skill in carrying out procedures flexibly, accurately, efficiently and appropriately.

Kilpatrick et al. (2001) believe that these five strands, woven together, are equal in importance, dependent on each other, represent the different aspects needed and necessary in supporting learners to be proficient in mathematics. We would also argue that they are just as applicable in science. Learners need to be able to use all of these strands to productively solve problems and investigations.

This book explores reasoning and the skills associated with it. But reasoning fits into the bigger picture of solving problems and investigations. The point of being able to use the **skills of reasoning** is to ultimately pose, engage with and solve problems and investigations.

This chapter links strongly to others; for example, Chapter 4 on questions. We might struggle to even approach mathematical problems or conduct science investigations systematically without mathematical or scientific questions. Equally, being able to predict (Chapter 5) or spot patterns (Chapter 6) are skills that learners will draw on when solving problems and engaging with investigations.

What do we mean by problem-solving and investigation?

The terms 'problem-solving' and 'investigation' can be used quite liberally, and in different ways. We have all probably heard phrases such as, We only do problem-solving on a Friday, or, Today we are going to do an investigation. This would suggest that problem-solving and investigations are nouns; activities that are contained and special, separate from other forms of learning.

Problem-solving and investigation can be umbrella terms that refer to an investigative process, or an inquiry, where learners are using skills and strategies to pursue some thinking and reasoning. But they can also be used in a narrow, specific way to mean the finite solution to a problem or indeed the focus of a lesson. However, our view is that problem-solving and investigation are at the very heart of mathematics and science and that everything we do is about solving a problem or engaging in an investigation.

Polya (1945) offered this definition. Problem-solving is:

- seeking solutions, not just memorising procedures;

- exploring patterns, not just memorising formulas;

- formulating conjectures, not just doing exercises.

Investigation is a broader term and can be suffixed as a mathematical investigation, scientific investigation or other. To investigate is to examine, to systematically inquire (Fowler and Fowler, 1984), thus it is a process which can occur in the full range of subject disciplines and human experience. Investigation is a term used by science educationalists, but terms like 'science inquiry' and 'science process' can also apply. Science investigations use science knowledge, understanding, skills and the science process to systematically plan science inquiries. In this chapter we will use the term investigation to refer to an investigation that could occur in mathematics or science.

These definitions offer approaches which are exploratory and increasingly systematic; they utilise and apply knowledge and skills, giving some freedom to the increasingly autonomous problem-solver/investigator to plan their approach. They are both tools that enable learners to make sense of what they are noticing or exploring. In some cases, this will be used in the big umbrella sense, but in other places it will also be focused on a particular inquiry.

So, perhaps it is important to say that we do not consider problem-solving and investigation to be about a set of rules that need to be memorised and repeated. If learners are waiting for the teacher to ask them a question or tell them how to solve a problem this suggests that mathematics and science are nothing more than a set of routines to follow. This is going to limit opportunities to use any of the **skills of reasoning** that we consider to be the currency of the future.

The importance of problem-solving and investigation in the future

As we suggested in Chapter 1, the currency of the future is changing. Learners will need a different set of skills as we move fowards in the twenty-first century. Already we are beginning to see more emphasis placed on the importance of STEM subjects and the associated skills they utilise. The importance of being STEM-literate and recognising individual mathematics or science (Godec et al., 2017) capital is increasing as we head for a shortage in our future workforce of people who will have these skills. This is not a new problem. In 1985 The Royal Society produced a report that warned of *hostility, or even indifference, to science and technology,* saying that this *weakens the nation's industry* (The Royal Society, 1985). It also suggested that this attitude appeared to be more common in Britain than in our major competitors of the time such as Germany, Japan or the United States. However, the report also made a good point that understanding the importance of science (and we would include mathematics here) is important on a personal level for all individuals, in making decisions involving health, diet and other factors that influence us all daily.

Yet, many learners (and adults) lack confidence and even exhibit anxiety towards mathematics and to a lesser extent science (Welcome Trust, 2017). There are many reasons for these negative attitudes but often it results from a belief or fear of failing at either subject. When asked, learners (and adults) will often comment that they are no good at fractions, division or understanding physics. Yet their comments rarely centre on their lack of being able to question, convince or explain. They have located their anxiety within the subject-specific part of each subject and not the skills that we have been exploring in this book. It is these skills that we need the learners of today to have in the future. Of course, there will always be a need to have some subject knowledge but there will be more of a necessity to have the skills. After all, computers will be able to store and recall the knowledge at the press of a button, thumbprint or recognition of a voice command. The **skills of reasoning** are part of our capacity to problem-solve and investigate.

Connecting mathematics and science through problem-solving and investigations

There are many ways in which mathematics and science link together through number, proportionality, pattern, measurement, geometry, statistics, working scientifically and working mathematically (Cross and Borthwick, 2016). Mathematics and science overlap so strongly that any dividing line is blurred. Many teachers have also welcomed the opportunity for enhancing links between subjects such as mathematics and science, recognising that such links inevitably draw on and develop skills for both subjects (DCSF/QCDA, 2010).

TRY THIS!

Ask learners to make links between mathematics and science. What do they see as the connections? Content? Skills?

For learners, solving a problem or an investigation is drawing on the same skill set whether the subject is mathematics or science. According to Haylock (2010) solving problems gives learners opportunities to *use logical reasoning, suggest solutions and try out different approaches to problems* (Haylock, 2010). When learners are challenged to tackle mathematics and science problems and investigations, they draw on very similar skills to do so. This chapter explores how the **skills of reasoning** support and enable learners to solve problems and investigations across both mathematics and science.

One of these skills, that we explored in depth in Chapter 4, was questioning. The ability to pose problems in the form of a question is an important skill and one that also assists learners when they are trying to solve problems and investigations.

We might consider whether there are times when these questions are initiated by the teacher. Are there times when these are best initiated by the learner? As learners become more experienced is there opportunity for them to take more responsibility?

REFLECTION

In your classroom, who is it who poses the questions which lead to problem-solving and investigation?

Is it you? Is it the learners?

Could the focus shift?

When approaching problems and questions to be investigated as a means of developing reasoning we might devote time to ensuring that the learners really do understand the problem or question. If they understand the context, perhaps engaging with a person or character facing the problem or question, they can begin to appreciate the need for thought and actions to find out more. If they are the ones who formulate the problem or question this is likely to assist them further.

One approach is to elicit a number of problems or questions from a class and involve them in selecting one or more to pursue. Another approach related to this is to take learner questions and prompt the learners to improve the question to make it into a better question, which can be investigated. Look at some examples below (Table 7.1).

Can you suggest improvements to the questions?

How could you prompt primary-aged learners to suggest improvements to questions so that they can be investigated mathematically or scientifically?

Table 7.1 Improving learners' initial questions

Question from class/learner	Better version?	Better still?
Which ball rolls best?	Which ball rolls furthest?	How does the size of the ball affect the distance it rolls?
Which coat is safe at night?	Which coat reflects most light?	Which material reflects the most light?
What do plants need?	What conditions do plants need to grow?	What is the effect on plant growth when we change the amount of light?
What is 3 + 4?	What pairs of numbers can be added to give 7?	What numbers when operated on result with the answer 7?
What is $\frac{1}{2}$ of 10?	How many ways can we halve 10?	What does halving mean?
Is a square a quadrilateral?	How many shapes can you think of that are quadrilaterals?	What are the properties of quadrilaterals?

TRY THIS!

In mathematics or science lessons ask learners to pose five questions on a topic, which could be investigated.

Then select one and coach them to improve the question.

Only when we have a good mathematical or scientific question can we then begin to design an effective strategy to solve or answer it and use the **skills of reasoning**. If learners had been given the initial question from those presented in Table 7.1 their problem-solving and investigating might have been short-lived.

If learners are to be mathematicians or scientists they are likely to benefit from the power of improving questions. In order for learners to improve a question, your prompts might include:

- What do we mean by best?

- What are the key words in our question?

- Are there more mathematical/scientific words we could use?

- Can we mention one thing that affects another thing?

- Are we asking about the right thing?

REFLECTION

Could learners assist each other with a critique of another's plans to investigate or solve a problem?

Could learners offer two stars and two wishes to help another learner identify strengths and aspects to develop a plan to solve a problem or conduct an investigation?

In order to move to problem-solving or investigating, learners then need to interrogate the question. There are ways that we as teachers scaffold learners' experience so as to shift control towards them and enable them as learners of mathematics and science. For example, we might model this by asking:

- What is being asked here?

- What do I already know?

- Can I make a prediction or offer a conjecture?

- How can my skills and knowledge assist me?

- How can I move forward now?

- How will I tackle the problem/question?

- Is this the best approach?

Different types of problems, investigations and strategies

Meaningful reasoning must revolve around a context, a place, a phenomenon, relationships, values, cause and effect, and more. A misconception (particularly in mathematics) is that problem-solving is only used when there is a real-life situation, or that it is only a problem when it is written down with lots of words. However, if we consider that everything we do in mathematics is about solving a problem, or that our purpose in science is to investigate, then we need to re-define our definition of problem-solving.

We offer two ways to consider how to re-think what we are doing when we are problem-solving. The first is to explore the different types of problems or investigations there are. The first list is perhaps more familiar to a mathematical context:

- word problems;

- visual problems;

- finding all possibilities;

- logic problems;

- rules and patterns.

The second list, perhaps more familiar to a science context, explores different types of investigations taken from Turner et al. (2011). As with mathematics, children learn from a range of different forms of investigative work – all of which enable and benefit from reasoning. Turner et al. advise a range of scientific investigations which encourages a broad and balanced approach to science investigation by learners (which we explore in Chapter 5). These investigations almost always require learners to think scientifically and to think mathematically (Cross and Borthwick, 2016):

- observing over time;

- identifying and classifying;

- pattern seeking;

- secondary research;

- comparative and fair testing.

Whether a problem is presented abstractedly (for example, 3 + 4?), in words (what is three add four?) or algebraically ($x + y$?) it is still a problem that we need to solve – so we need to look beyond the problem and consider what type of problem it is. Every problem draws on **skills of reasoning** that we have been offering throughout this book. Some of these skills will be common to many of the problems; others will lend themselves more to one than another.

Alongside different types of problems there are also different strategies involved in solving problems. Examples include:

- pattern spotting;

- grouping and classifying;

- working systematically;

- using diagrams and pictorial information;

- working backwards;

- predicting, conjecturing and hypothesising;

- trial and improvement;

- visualising;

- gathering and interpreting evidence;

- generalising;

- using manipulatives/equipment.

Some of these strategies are also **skills of reasoning** (for example, conjecturing and visualising), but others remain a discrete strategy that we might employ to solve a problem (for example, working systematically). However, both the types of problems and problem-solving strategies require **skills of reasoning** (as well as other elements, as Kilpatrick et al., 2001 suggest) to successfully solve a problem. Table 7.2 offers some examples to illustrate this.

Table 7.2 Reasoning skills matched to types of problems and problem-solving strategies

Types of problems/investigations/ problem-solving strategy	Possible skills of reasoning
word problems	deconstructing, decoding, explaining
visual problems	visualising, noticing, wondering
finding all possibilities	organising, being systematic, being logical
logic problems	questioning, organising, refuting
rules and patterns	noticing, recognising links, pattern seeking
observation over time	pattern seeking, noticing, extrapolating
identifying and classifying	comparing, organising, convincing
research (using secondary sources)	making connections, decoding, noticing
comparative testing	predicting, being systematic, organising
fair testing	decomposing, justifying, visualising

(Continued)

Table 7.2 (Continued)

Types of problems/investigations/ problem-solving strategy	Possible skills of reasoning
pattern seeking/spotting	tinkering, speculating, deleting
grouping and classifying	making connections, pattern seeking, comparing
working systematically	organising, making connections, justifying
using diagrams and pictorial information	visualising, comparing, proving
working backwards	decomposing, working backwards, verifying
trial and improvement	offering counter examples, correcting
visualising	visualising, noticing, wondering
predicting, conjecturing and hypothesising	specialising, generalising, wondering
gathering and interpreting evidence	organising, interpolating, making judgements
generalising	conjecturing, specialising, offering counter examples
using manipulatives/equipment	organising, interpolating, describing

As we consider a context, a problem, a question or an investigation we begin to deploy our **skills of reasoning**.

The process of problem-solving and investigation

How we solve a problem in mathematics or pursue an investigation in science may differ in the words we use or the approach we take. However, they still require the same **skills of reasoning**. We offer two examples below; the first is taken from a mathematical content and the second from a scientific one.

Woodham (2014) suggests a four-stage process to solving a problem.

(1) getting started

(2) working on the problem

(3) digging deeper

(4) concluding

Within each of these stages various **skills of reasoning** will be used. For example, in the first stage learners may need to decode the problem and begin to notice and puzzle over what to do. By the fourth stage learners may now be proving, convincing and justifying to themselves and to their peers.

Scientists will recognise the process below (Figure 7.2) as a familiar way to approach a science investigation.

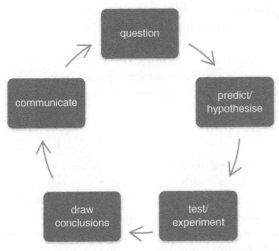

Figure 7.2 The science process

Each step in the science process has potential for scientific (and mathematical) thinking, and thus reasoning. For example, What measure should I use? Will this allow me to gather data which will help me answer the question? Is this a cycle that we share with learners? Can we emphasise the choices, thought and justification which go on at each stage?

While the stages may look different to the one suggested by Woodham (2014), learners could still be using the same **skills of reasoning** such as decoding the question, noticing and puzzling over their predictions or proving that their hypothesis was correct.

REASONING FOCUS

Looking at Figures 7.2 and 7.3 can you see parts of each process that are more likely to enable reasoning?

Collaborative problem-solving and investigation

Most adults, when asked, prefer to solve mathematical or scientific problems collaboratively, yet this is often undervalued in classrooms, particularly mathematical ones. Recent reports (for example, Luckin et al., 2017) have strongly encouraged schools and teachers to increase the provision for collaborative problem-solving, and evidence gathered confirms that the skills that collaborative problem-solving draw on are *both ancient and yet very relevant to the future* (Luckin et al., 2017).

In 2017 the OECD published its first country rankings for collaborative problem-solving, recognising that these skills are becoming more important as we head towards the rest of the twenty-first century (OECD, 2017). There are different definitions for collaborative problem-solving, which all revolve around learners solving problems together, but the one provided by the OECD (2015) is even more specific.

> *The capacity of an individual to effectively engage in a process whereby two or more agents attempt to solve a problem by sharing the understanding and effort required to come to a solution and pooling their knowledge, skills and efforts to reach that solution.*

(OECD, 2015)

Collaborative problem-solving and investigation chimes with the guidance we are offering on reasoning and the skills associated with it. In Chapter 1 we suggested that while learners can reason on their own, this limits the skills they will potentially use. This is the same for solving problems and investigations. Being able to work collaboratively provides an opportunity for learners to draw on **skills of reasoning** such as agreeing and disagreeing, describing, explaining and convincing, that they may not otherwise have opportunities to do. While there are other requirements involved with collaborative problem-solving (for example, choice of task, group responsibility, reflection) this approach provides an ideal link to reasoning and the skills we are exploring.

Increasing autonomy in learners to pose their own problems or investigations

Allowing learners to develop autonomy in investigation and problem-solving can increase the challenge of the activity because learners have to use their **skills of reasoning**.

Learners planning a fair test, for example, need to be clear about the question. Can they suggest an approach to solving or investigating the question? In order to tackle these questions learners must reason.

Some teachers and schools use writing frames (Figure 7.3) to assist planning and recording of science investigations. These have real potential to enable reasoning about science investigations and could easily be used in mathematics, too.

Many primary science writing frames adopt a format which identifies the question, the change and measure variables, a prediction and results framed in the language of the change and measure variable (Goldsworthy and Feasey, 1997). These are powerful for enabling features for reasoning as they encourage the control of variables and the identification of cause and effect in the change and measurement of variables. Such formats allow us as teachers to emphasise the features of an investigation and to draw attention to how the change variable influences (or not) the variable being observed or measured. For example, as we change the temperature of water we see a change in the amount of salt which will dissolve in it. As learners observe the results they can reason and consider whether a pattern has emerged, whether their prediction has proved

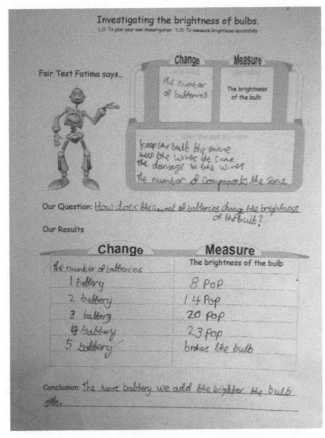

Figure 7.3 Science investigation writing frame (pop = pieces of paper)

correct, whether their original question has been answered and whether they might pose further questions.

Using errors to enable reasoning skills

One class studying thermal insulation set up an investigation with different materials (the change variable) wrapped around identical yoghurt pots containing warm water. They measured the temperature of the pots every five minutes to observe which materials prevented temperature reduction. Their results can be seen in Table 7.3.

Their question – Which material is the best thermal insulator?

Their prediction – Foil will be the best thermal insulator.

Table 7.3 Results from an investigation of the thermal insulation of different materials

Time (mins)	Pot 1 Bubble wrap	Pot 2 Felt	Pot 3 Foil	Pot 4 Paper	Pot 5 No insulation
0	58 degrees	58 degrees	58 degrees	58 degrees	58 degrees
5	56 degrees	56 degrees	55 degrees	56 degrees	54 degrees
10	55 degrees	54 degrees	54 degrees	52 degrees	51 degrees
15	53 degrees	51 degrees	50 degrees	49 degrees	47 degrees
20	51 degrees	47 degrees	47 degrees	46 degrees	42 degrees
25	48 degrees	44 degrees	45 degrees	43 degrees	38 degrees
30	47 degrees	42 degrees	43 degrees	40 degrees	40 degrees
35	46 degrees	39 degrees	40 degrees	37 degrees	42 degrees

The tests had been carried out in a systematic way but the results in the right-hand column (Pot 5) appeared anomalous. The temperature appeared to have dropped, then risen. Initially the learners accepted these results; they had been systematic, they had used thermometers, their visiting science specialist teacher had been on hand: results are results, they must be right. After a prompt from the teacher, the class realised that there was something wrong. Asked for an explanation they questioned the learner taking the readings and the quality of the thermometer (they were considering experimental error). No one had noticed that the Sun had begun to shine through the window onto Pot 5 and had warmed the pot (experimental error). They could then explain the results which, as ever, told the story of what had happened. The learners quickly suggested a number of ways to overcome this problem.

However, this example reveals that allowing learners to make errors provides an additional platform for their **skills of reasoning** to develop. In this lesson learners noticed, questioned, wondered, worked backwards, explained, justified, refuted and altered their conclusions. They required quite a string of skills from their reasoning toolkit in order to correct their error. It would have been very easy for the teacher to step in and adjust, but this would have limited the opportunities for reasoning. In this example, the errors allowed learners to develop their **skills of reasoning** further.

The following section explores some activities that we can use, under the umbrella of problem-solving and investigation, that also draw on a variety of **skills of reasoning**.

— TEACHING ACTIVITY —

Skills of reasoning: noticing, observing, predicting, comparing, pattern seeking

Investigations over time can be very strong in terms of mathematics and science knowledge and skill development. These often occur in aspects of biology, including animal and plant growth.

Learners can grow seeds measuring and observing the growth of the stem. They can investigate questions about the conditions for growth. For example:

What is the effect on plant growth of different growing mediums (soil)?

What is the effect on plant growth of the place we grow them?

What is the effect on plant growth of the temperature?

What is the effect on plant growth given the amount of watering?

Typically, such investigations take place over a week or two and allow for questioning, prediction, observation, measurement, recording on tables and graphs, pattern seeking, results, conclusions and communication.

Figure 7.4 Testing the growth of seedlings

TEACHING ACTIVITY

Skills of reasoning: specialising, generalising, organising, conjecturing

Ask learners to choose any three consecutive numbers and add them together. For example:

3, 4, 5   22, 23, 24   98, 99, 100   45, 46, 47

After they have tried a few examples, ask learners what they notice.

This is a great problem to begin exploring generic proof. Learners may begin to notice that the sum of adding three consecutive numbers is always a multiple of three, or that the total is always three times the middle number, but can they explain why?

TEACHING ACTIVITY

Skills of reasoning: noticing, justifying, organising, using logic, specialising, sorting and classifying

Learners and primary teachers cannot be expected to identify all plants, animals and materials they may encounter. Learners can learn the names of locally occurring common plants and animals and commonly encountered materials. Perhaps more usefully, they can learn to group and classify and to use identification keys.

Can you group sweets and perhaps create a branching key to identify them?

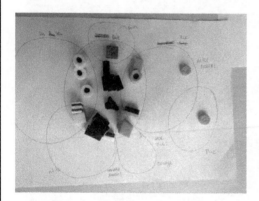 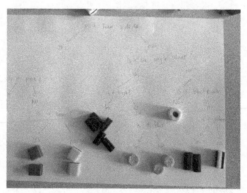

Figure 7.5 Classification of sweets

Can the learners justify their grouping? Add additional sweets to the groups? Form new groups?

Find simple identification keys and guides (trees, seaweed, ferns, etc.) at **www.opalexplorenature. org/identification.**

TEACHING ACTIVITY

Skills of reasoning: sorting, organising, noticing, explaining, convincing, proving

Set the scene: You and eleven friends go out for pizza. You order eight pizzas that you need to share between you equally. How much pizza does each person get?

With this question, encourage learners to draw or use equipment to help them to solve the problem. Encourage the learners to consider more than one way of sharing out the pizza.

Can they explain if they might prefer $\frac{1}{2} + \frac{1}{6}$ of a pizza, compared to $\frac{2}{3}$ of a pizza?

TEACHING ACTIVITY

Skills of reasoning: evaluating, convincing, verifying, organising, explaining, questioning, recognising links, agreeing, disagreeing

Humans have already learned a great deal about the world and increasingly we use familiar search engines and websites to answer questions and find out more. It may be that reasoning is becoming our most valuable guard against misinformation: there may be a danger if we are unaware of the range of information that is available from different sources, some of which is more reliable than others. Children should learn to use a range of secondary sources, including books and websites, and consider how trustworthy sources are.

Can learners generate questions they would like to answer about space?

Is *Star Wars* real?

Why is the Sun in space?

Why can't we see the Moon all the time?

Can they use this grid to arrange their questions down the left-hand column and then note evidence found in a range of sources?

	https://solarsystem.nasa.gov/planets	The Usborne Book of Astronomy & Space	DK Space	The First Big Book of Space
Where does the Moon go at night?				
Is there alien life in space?				

(Continued)

(Continued)

	https://solarsystem.nasa.gov/planets	The Usborne Book of Astronomy & Space	DK Space	The First Big Book of Space
What is an eclipse?				
How old is space?				

Can learners now give short summary answers to their questions?

Children can learn a great deal about mathematics and science, the nature of both subjects and working mathematically and scientifically by learning about the lives and discoveries of mathematicians and scientists. Learning about how these mathematicians and scientists made observations, predictions, conjectures, investigations, etc. can give a real sense of reasoning about the world.

Could learners research the observations made by Charles Darwin of animals in the Galapagos Islands? What is it that made him think? Reason? What did he observe? Are there times when we look at the world and ask questions?

TEACHING ACTIVITY

Skills of reasoning: observing, speculating, organising, sorting, pattern seeking

Learners will need two dice to solve this problem.

In pairs, ask learners to roll two dice and add the numbers that are on the top together. Ask them if they think they will be able to make other totals. How many? Are there any totals that they cannot make? Why not?

Figure 7.6 Two dice

This investigation encourages learners to find all the possibilities while using their reasoning skills to spot patterns and notice any totals that are missing.

TEACHING ACTIVITY

Skills of reasoning: predicting, observing, making connections, working abstractly, agreeing/disagreeing

For many learners the most enjoyable part of science is when they conduct tests and experiments. The simplest of these are trial and error tests and observations. As children learn about mathematics and science they can become more systematic in selecting and designing tests to answer a specific question. As we have seen in Chapter 4, reasoning can begin with a question. It can continue here as the learner suggests a test, is able to justify this, makes a prediction, carries out the test, observes or measures the result, then reconsiders the question asked and how they will now proceed.

Learners might compare a host of different things:

the strength of different materials;

the brightness of electrical bulbs;

the distance travelled by paper darts;

the growth of different seeds;

the sound of different musical instruments;

the transparency of different materials;

friction caused by different surfaces.

Some of these are observed with the senses (qualitative measures); others are measured with numbers – for example, decibels (quantitative measures).

TEACHING ACTIVITY

Skills of reasoning: being logical, deconstructing, noticing, puzzling, decomposing, sorting, organising, pattern seeking

Giving learners tasks that they need to puzzle over and wonder about is a great way to enable lots of **skills of reasoning**.

For this problem learners will need to be confident in using hundred squares. Here is one example of a hundred square.

(Continued)

(Continued)

1	2	3	4	5	6	7	8	9	10
11	12	13	14	15	16	17	18	19	20
21	22	23	24	25	26	27	28	29	30
31	32	33	34	35	36	37	38	39	40
41	42	43	44	45	46	47	48	49	50
51	52	53	54	55	56	57	58	59	60
61	62	63	64	65	66	67	68	69	70
71	72	73	74	75	76	77	78	79	80
81	82	83	84	85	86	87	88	89	90
91	92	93	94	95	96	97	98	99	100

Figure 7.7 An example of a hundred square

Give learners numbers from 1 to 100, but written in a different language, and ask them to decide where the numbers would fit onto a hundred square. What skills are learners using to decode the numbers? Have they spotted any patterns between the numbers?

Why not use Chinese numbers, Roman numerals, Arabic numbers?

TEACHING ACTIVITY

Skills of reasoning: questioning, predicting, justifying, organising, noticing, visualising, predicting, being logical, refuting, being systematic

It is important in science that learners move towards more and more systematic forms of testing. In primary education we tend to work towards what we call 'fair testing' where learners change one variable and observe or measure one variable. The test is considered fair if other variables are controlled and kept the same.

Could you design a fair test to answer this question?

Which material wrapped around an ice cube will prevent the ice from melting the longest?

Figure 7.8 Keeping ice solid

Can learners select from a range of sensing equipment? Do they know what unit to use? Can they justify their choices? Would a Datalogger provide more data faster? Given that a Datalogger produces a graph quickly, would this assist our search for pattern?

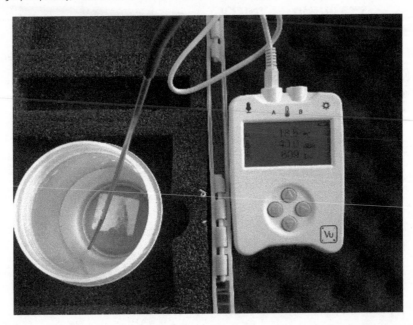

Figure 7.9 A Datalogger

(Data Harvest Ltd. Vu Datalogger)

TEACHING ACTIVITY

Skills of reasoning: working backwards, specialising, recognising links, noticing, correcting

Think of a rule and ask learners to suggest numbers to test the rule.

Here are some examples of rules you might choose:

All the numbers are odd numbers.

All the numbers are below 33.

All the numbers are multiples of 4.

All the numbers are square numbers.

All the numbers are between 20 and 30.

All the numbers have the digit 3 in them.

After you have made sure learners understand the game, limit them to the amount of numbers they can suggest. This begins to draw on different **skills of reasoning** as they begin to think more carefully about which numbers to suggest.

Finally, ask learners to make up their own rules and test them out on each other.

TEACHING ACTIVITY

Skills of reasoning: noticing, pattern seeking, questioning, making judgements

Using secondary sources is another way to engage learners in investigations and uses different **skills of reasoning** than if they were planning and carrying out the investigation themselves.

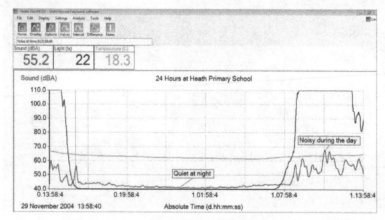

Figure 7.10 Screenshot from Datalogging software showing temperature, light and sound in a classroom over 24 hours (13:59 day 0 to 13:58 day 1)

(Courtesy of Data Harvest Ltd)

Software designed for Dataloggers allows the user to label the graph to emphasise patterns and features, and enable reasoning about the graph. Questions posed by a teacher can require straightforward reading of the graph and progressively deeper reasoning. For example:

What was the measure of sound at 07:58?

Why was the level of sound so low for so long?

Could the school save money on heating? If so, how?

If a burglar broke into the classroom at night, how might the graph change?

Would you expect the same data every night of the week?

TEACHING ACTIVITY

Skills of reasoning: being systematic, organising, being logical, sorting, pattern seeking

Hannah has 1p coins, 2p coins, 5p coins and 10p coins. How many different ways can Hannah make 30p? How will she know she has them all?

Figure 7.11 Coins

CHAPTER SUMMARY

This chapter has demonstrated how reasoning fits into the bigger picture of solving problems and investigations. It has shown that the point of being able to use the **skills of reasoning** is to ultimately pose, engage with and solve problems, and design and carry out mathematics and science investigations.

Having read this chapter you will:

- understand the place of problem-posing, problem-solving and investigating in promoting reasoning;
- be familiar with several examples of each;
- understand that pupil autonomy when investigating and solving problems has the potential to enhance opportunities for reasoning;
- have a bank of activities to use within a problem-solving and investigation context that enables learners to use their reasoning skills;
- know how problem-solving and investigation contributes to the **skills of reasoning**.

8

NOTICING AND EVIDENCING REASONING

IN THIS CHAPTER

By the end of this chapter you will:

- have a variety of ways to collect evidence of learners' reasoning;
- understand the different ways that learners can show how they are reasoning;
- be able to recognise that learners who are using skills such as justifying, generalising and proving have reached a peak of logical, purposeful, goal-orientated reasoning.

Introduction

We may have previously thought of reasoning as a separate, isolated activity; perhaps an extension to thinking, used to solve a problem. However, as the previous seven chapters have shown, reasoning is central to learning about mathematics and science. Not only is it a form of thinking which helps us to solve problems, it is also a skill that we draw on continually to help us make sense of the world. How do we know a square is a square and not a circle, or that these materials will float while others sink?

Often, because these ideas are so obvious and familiar to us we forget that we are reasoning. It is hard to notice something when we barely register the cognitive activity. Yet we are still using our **skills of reasoning** in these situations. So, if we as adults find it difficult to notice when we are reasoning, it becomes even harder to spot when learners are doing it.

This chapter considers two different ways in which we can notice and then evidence reasoning by learners. The first way is one that we are regularly asked about: How can we provide evidence of reasoning with the work that learners produce? We will explore the different media, such as written work, photographs, drawings, etc. and offer some suggestions for teachers to try. However, the second way is more fundamental. It considers the importance of learners developing hallmarks of reasoning that allow them to improve and refine their reasoning. Once learners have noticed a pattern, offered a conjecture or made a prediction, then the next step is to gather evidence to either prove or disprove their reasoning. This will encourage learners to begin convincing, justifying and generalising. Learners should observe if examples appear to have commonalities in them, which will help them to consider if a generalisation can be made and ask, Will this always work?

One more point: it is popularly believed that learners need to be taught 'basic' skills in both mathematics and science before they can reason, solve problems or generalise. We do not find this to be the case. All learners, whatever their age, can and do reason. So, this chapter is applicable to all learners, at whatever stage in their education they are at.

TRY THIS!

I cannot teach anybody anything; I can only make them think.

Discuss this quote from Socrates with colleagues and also learners. What do they think?

Why is it important to evidence reasoning?

The different and multifaceted ways in which learners understand ideas in mathematics and science are intriguing. Often learners see things in very different ways to adults and this needs to be celebrated. Collecting any sort of evidence, whether it is of learners reasoning, or any other aspect of the curriculum, must be a worthwhile and reasonable activity to do. However, for many, education has become a world of accountability – whether this is through the outcomes of tests, external bodies making judgements about schools or simply the pressures to prove what we are teaching and what our learners are learning. In your context these may be perceived to be necessary. However, we would not want learners to begin to associate their competencies in reasoning with a grade, number or letter. Such a crude representation is not helpful and learners may begin to define themselves by it.

There is another, better reason to evidence reasoning. Firstly, we want learners to reason because it improves their understanding. In a four-year study of different schools, Boaler (2016) discovered that reasoning had a particular role to play in the promotion of equity. Being able to reason helped to reduce the gap between students who understood and students who were struggling. Skills such as reasoning are becoming the currency of the future, as more and more employers are looking for students who have the ability to think and reason, rather than simply recall facts and regurgitate knowledge (The Royal Society, 2014).

It is also important for teachers to know about each learner's capacity to reason so they can support and scaffold further developments. Formative assessment, otherwise known as assessment for learning, is useful in finding out where children are in their learning so that teachers and learners can determine what they need to do next. Using evidence can also highlight any misconceptions learners may have about mathematical or scientific knowledge.

A particularly important principle of assessment for learning is about empowering learners to be reflective about their learning. This allows them to focus on understanding, rather than activity, and utilises some of the reasoning characteristics we have explored in this book. In the lessons we observed where reasoning was a focus we noticed learners engaged in rich dialogue about their learning. Learners were positively encouraged to talk about and discuss their learning with the teacher and their peers. They shared a responsibility for their learning and understanding and as a result they asked questions, considered alternative viewpoints and made connections.

REFLECTION

How do we really know if learners are reasoning? What characteristics do they exhibit?

In Chapter 1 we referred to all the science in the learner's life as their science capital (Godec et al., 2017) and all the mathematics in their life as mathematics capital. Reasoning adds significantly to this and the ideas that follow are ones that reveal portions of this capital.

Are two subjects better than one to support the evidence of reasoning?

We have shown (Cross and Borthwick, 2016) that the skills we draw on for mathematics and science overlap considerably. While the subject content remains discrete, many of the skills we draw on are identical. This is also true for the **skills of reasoning**. While we believe that reasoning is at the heart of both mathematics and science, it is also providing learners with a lifelong skill and preparing them for the high-tech world in which they will be working. You might reflect on whether reasoning is one of the hallmarks of human thought.

With two subjects there are twice as many opportunities to provide reasoning activities, and twice as many opportunities to observe and reflect on how well learners are reasoning.

Two different subjects allow the application and transference of skills and act as a model for transfer then to the wider range of STEM and other subjects and activities.

REFLECTION

Do we collect evidence to support learners further, or because we need to show evidence of reasoning?

Different ways to evidence reasoning

Reasoning may be perceived to be hard to evidence because it is considered to be an internal, silent action. However, we hope the previous seven chapters have shown you that reasoning is constantly revealed in learner behaviour and speech; for example, questioning, predicting, pattern spotting and problem-solving. The following section explores different ways that reasoning can be externalised and captured.

Collecting evidence through drawings or pictures

Using drawings to gather data has proved a powerful catalyst in creating conversations with teachers about their practice and how learners view mathematics and science lessons in their classrooms (Borthwick, 2008). So, using drawings to collect evidence from learners about their reasoning is a logical step. It is also an effective way to harness all contributions from learners.

Using drawings adds a visual component to learners' understanding, which can enhance learning for many children. As Boaler writes, *when students are stuck in maths class, I often ask them to draw the problem out* (Boaler, 2016); while Ryan and Williams (2007) say that, *a picture is sometimes worth a thousand words*. This is because drawings and pictures can provide the basis for understanding mathematical and scientific strategies and conceptions. However, like any piece of evidence, other triangulation of evidence may need to be sought through questioning, talking or explaining further.

The example in Figure 8.1 shows how one learner has used a drawing of an array (sometimes called the bar model) to support their understanding of how to multiply fractions by fractions. Using a diagram for this piece of mathematics allowed the learner to see how common denominators are created, rather than just being taught the trick of multiplying the denominators together. In one example the calculation is $\frac{1}{2} \times \frac{1}{3}$. The child has drawn a block and then divided it into two parts horizontally, and then divided the same block into three parts vertically. This has produced a 2×3 grid, resulting in six squares. By shading in one half and one third so that they cross over, you can now notice the part which is shaded twice, therefore revealing the answer ($\frac{1}{6}$).

When talking to the teacher about this piece of work she said that the whole class had really struggled with understanding how to multiply fractions by fractions. They had previously used an abstract method (multiplying the numerators and denominators together) but with little understanding as to why this revealed the correct answer. However, since they had begun to scaffold their understanding through drawing blocks, all the learners were more successful in achieving the correct answer, and were also beginning to see the reasoning behind the mathematics.

Boaler (2016) also encourages learners to use colour-coding if applicable in their pictures, to help them to notice relationships and make connections. This is another way of representing ideas in different ways. For example, one of the tasks she uses is about colour-coding a tray of brownies. In this task Sam needs to work out how 24 brownies could be shared equally between himself and five friends. Colour-coding the brownies allows the different ways they can be shared to be recorded, rather than just providing the answer of four each.

Collecting evidence through photographs and video

One of the advantages in using photographs and video as a source of evidence is that both learners and adults can participate in this. Most schools have multiple ways to harness technology through

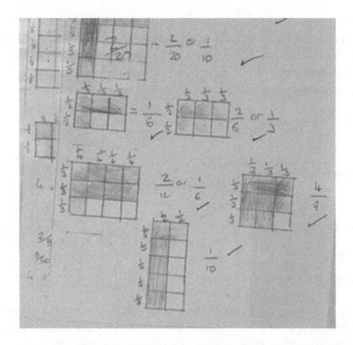

Figure 8.1 Learners use drawings to understand how to multiply fractions by fractions

devices such as tablet computers, cameras, etc.; often learners are more skilled than adults with this technology and so we can use this to our advantage (Computing at School, 2013).

Figure 8.2 An annotated photograph from a lesson records learners' thinking

(Cross and Board, 2014)

153

Photographs and video can capture any stage of the reasoning process. Figure 8.2 is an annotated photograph which illustrates 10-year-old learners reasoning about push and pull forces in a tug of war. In a photograph, learners are transported back to that activity, that moment. They can rekindle the interest, the challenge, the reasoning and thinking. Questions posed in this lesson by the teacher and learners included:

Show me how you are pulling?

What is it that means you can pull?

Is this like strongest man in the world?

Is the push and pull the same?

She's pushing really hard.

Can you feel the pull and the push?

What would happen if you tried this on an ice rink?

Using photographs also draws on a part of the technological world that learners will need to be increasingly familiar and confident with. As teachers we want our learners to be digitally literate so they can be active participants in a digital world (Computing at School, 2013: 5).

Collecting evidence through learners' talking

Learners' talk is a source of evidence and, as we have said, a powerful medium for reasoning (aloud). Alexander (2008) recognises the power of talk for learning (see Chapter 1) and suggests that collaborative pupil talk for learning be a central focus of lessons. Perhaps this might be reasoning talk, or as Reznitskaya (2012) stated, a co-construction of ideas.

When evidencing reasoning through talk, it is important to distinguish between learners talking *about* mathematics or science and learners *talking* mathematics or science. There is a difference, just as there is a difference between talking about Spanish and talking Spanish. Try to notice if learners are making connections between their ideas, as opposed to a list of words describing the activity.

Yes, if the material has layers of air in it, it will keep things warm but does that mean it would keep cold things cold?

Productive talk about what is being learned is a rich pool of data, yet one of the most difficult sources to tangibly evidence. It can involve two or more people, and is built up through the exchange of ideas and thoughts. There are many ways to involve learners in talking. Perhaps one of the easiest is to use pair or partner talk. Asking learners to turn to their partner and talk requires little organisation and ensures everyone is involved.

Any of the reasoning scaffolds that we explored in Chapter 2 could be used to evidence how learners are reasoning through talk. For example, can learners describe, explain or convince their partner about something (part of the NRICH scaffold)? Can they wonder or pose questions (part of the 'See, Think, Wonder' scaffold)?

Another source of evidence is to observe and notice the quality of vocabulary that learners draw on. You might find it helpful to keep a list of reasoning skills, such as the ones we offered in Chapter 2 (see Table 8.1). Tick/highlight/initial if you hear learners using any of these words. You might like to keep individual records or a class checklist. With either, repeat multiple times over the course of the year and notice if the quantity of words learners are using increases.

Table 8.1   Suggested skills of reasoning

convincing	working abstractly	decomposing	interpolating	evaluating
being logical	hypothesising	extrapolating	proving	predicting
deconstructing	generalising	speculating	explaining	agreeing/ disagreeing
questioning	noticing	describing	justifying	making connections
recognising links	being systematic	making judgements	pattern seeking	exemplifying
comparing	doing/undoing	organising	refuting	tinkering
correcting	altering	specialising	verifying	deleting
offering counter examples	visualising	working backwards	wondering	puzzling
classifying	observing	sorting	conjecturing	playing

Using reasoning stems are helpful in scaffolding learners but are also a great source of evidencing reasoning through talk. You could make some speech bubbles like the ones below; add in phrases such as:

- I noticed that …

- I wondered if …?

- I used … strategy to work it out.

- When I was stuck …

- When I saw this, it made me think …

and then give these to learners to aid their reasoning. You might even like to select particular speech bubbles and allocate them to specific learners or pairs to feed back on their learning.

Rubrics are another scaffold that can support learners' reasoning. These provide useful signposts as to how learners are developing their talking and reasoning skills. Askew (2012) offers the following rubric to support whole-class, public conversations:

- rehearse

- revoice

- repeat

- rephrase

- build on

- comment on

Rehearse: This is an opportunity for children to practise what they are going to say out loud. It sets the expectation that they are required to talk, but gives them warning and time to rehearse.

Revoice: This part acts as an opportunity for children to see what it is like talking in front of others. It also gives the teacher the opportunity to ask for clarity, or re-model some of the talk.

Repeat: Asking children to repeat what their peers have said is quite revealing and shows that the art of talking is also good listening!

Rephrase: Once everyone has agreed on what has been said, ask children to explain what they have heard in their own words.

Build on: Offering children the opportunity to add anything, repeat or rephrase helps to clarify any gaps in understanding.

Comment on: A final opportunity to open out the dialogue and invite more discussion, ideas or comments.

Remember, too, that while learners are talking, you can also record a response in their books, which helps to capture the evidence. The example in Figure 8.3 highlights just this.

Similarly, try to capture whole-class discussions where learners reveal aspects of reasoning characteristics. In a mathematics lesson, learners are shown a hundred square (1–100) with the square

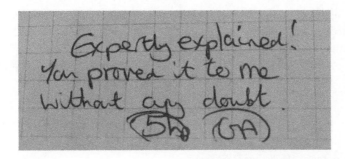

Figure 8.3 Evidence of learners' reasoning through talk

numbers shaded (1, 4, 9, 16, 25, 36, 49, 64, 81, 100). They are asked what they notice. Comments included:

It's not a pattern.

There's no 7 digit highlighted.

There's a hundred squares.

Figure 8.4 Whole-class comments

However you collect evidence of reasoning through talk, the important points to note are that a skillful teacher promotes reasoning through the choice of task (Swan, 2006), has the skill to accept and value what all learners say, and then the ability to scaffold this talk into constructive dialogue.

Most tasks can be approached in different ways. For example, a task that asks, How many ways …? might be more successful at inviting learners to describe, explain, convince and prove than a task which asks for a single answer.

Collecting evidence through using equipment

While there is a general agreement that using equipment in both mathematics and science is helpful (some may say essential), can it provide a useful medium to collect evidence of learners' reasoning in both subjects? Perhaps the focus of this question depends on whether teachers and learners see why and how using equipment is helpful for learning. As many educationalists would argue (e.g., Barmby et al., 2009; Kaput, 1992), it is not the piece of equipment that is important, but the way it is used to support understanding. This is the same for reasoning. Using equipment is a step towards understanding and reasoning, not just simply a tool presented to learners for them to use, without thought. For example, giving learners base ten equipment is not a guarantee that they will understand place value, nor is using a thermometer a guarantee of understanding temperature.

The use of equipment or manipulatives was justified by Bruner's (1966) formulation of three modes of communication to support understanding: the enactive mode (involving direct manipulation of materials); the iconic mode (involving images and pictures of those materials); and the symbolic mode (words, numbers and signs). Bruner's approach was inspired by Piaget's (1958) theory that a mental schema is the result of internalising an external action on objects.

In Figure 8.5 learners have been given multilink cubes to investigate square numbers. To begin with they explore what a square number 'looks' like by arranging the cubes into squares. To clarify: to square a number is to multiply it by itself. In other words, it is the product of an integer multiplied by itself. Quite quickly the learners begin to see that not all numbers can be square numbers. Using the cubes allows learners to begin to describe, explain and convince with each other. Some of them even begin to offer a proof using the equipment as support. The teacher asks them, Is eight a square number? No, because, see, you can't make a square, because you need the same number of cubes across as well as down.

Other comments included:

> That's not a square number. It's not equal. It's five across and six down.
>
> 150 is not a square number because there is no number that you can times by it to get that number.
>
> To get a square number I need to times the number by that number.

Figure 8.5 Exploring square numbers using multilink cubes

TRY THIS!

If learners are interested and can explain what a square number is, ask them to offer reasons as to what a happy number might be.

A happy number is ...

Collecting evidence through role-play

Using role-play as a pedagogical technique gives you permission to place learners in different roles that they may not otherwise assume. One strategy that has many benefits is asking learners to be skeptical of their friends (Mason, 1999). Explain to learners that there are three levels of convincing:

- convince yourself;
- convince a friend;
- convince a skeptic.

It is fairly easy to convince yourself or a friend, but you need different levels and **skills of reasoning** to convince a skeptic. Pair learners together and allocate roles of either convincer or skeptic. Explain that when it is their turn to be the skeptic, they need to be fully convinced.

Remind them that they require reasons and justifications that make sense. In our experience learners really enjoy challenging each other and are often hard task masters! As a teacher you may need to model what a fully convincing answer is, by asking follow-up questions if they have not been convincing enough. You may like to capture the evidence through filming the learners, noting down key words they use, giving them a score about how convincing they are or taking photographs as they are in full flow.

You might find that in attempting to offer a convincing argument, learners draw on other mediums such as the use of equipment, high levels of vocabulary or pictures.

Here are some activities to ask learners to convince a skeptic on:

- Convince your partner that the Moon moves around the Sun, and not the other way around.
- Convince your partner that $\frac{2}{4} < \frac{3}{4}$.
- Convince your partner that a magnetic force can travel through thin materials.
- Convince your partner that a square only has four right angles.

Collecting evidence through written work

This is probably the most common and frequently used medium for evidencing reasoning. Evidence can be collected by observing how learners have approached tasks; for example, through their choice of method or how they have organised their results. Teachers can also take opportunities to write questions to learners about their reasoning, as the example in Figure 8.6 below shows, and invite learners to offer their reasons.

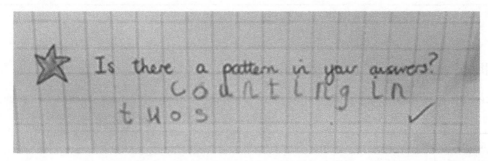

Figure 8.6 Evidence of learners' reasoning in response to a question from the teacher

Over time you can teach learners how to record their reasoning alongside work in their books. Using scaffolds such as the reasoning stems really helps here. In Figure 8.7, learners were asked to investigate how to convert improper fractions and mixed numbers. Having completed the problem they were then asked to notice any patterns. One learner wrote, I noticed that the first number got halved as it got to the end of the chart and it goes like this ½, 1, 1½, 2 and 2½ and so on.

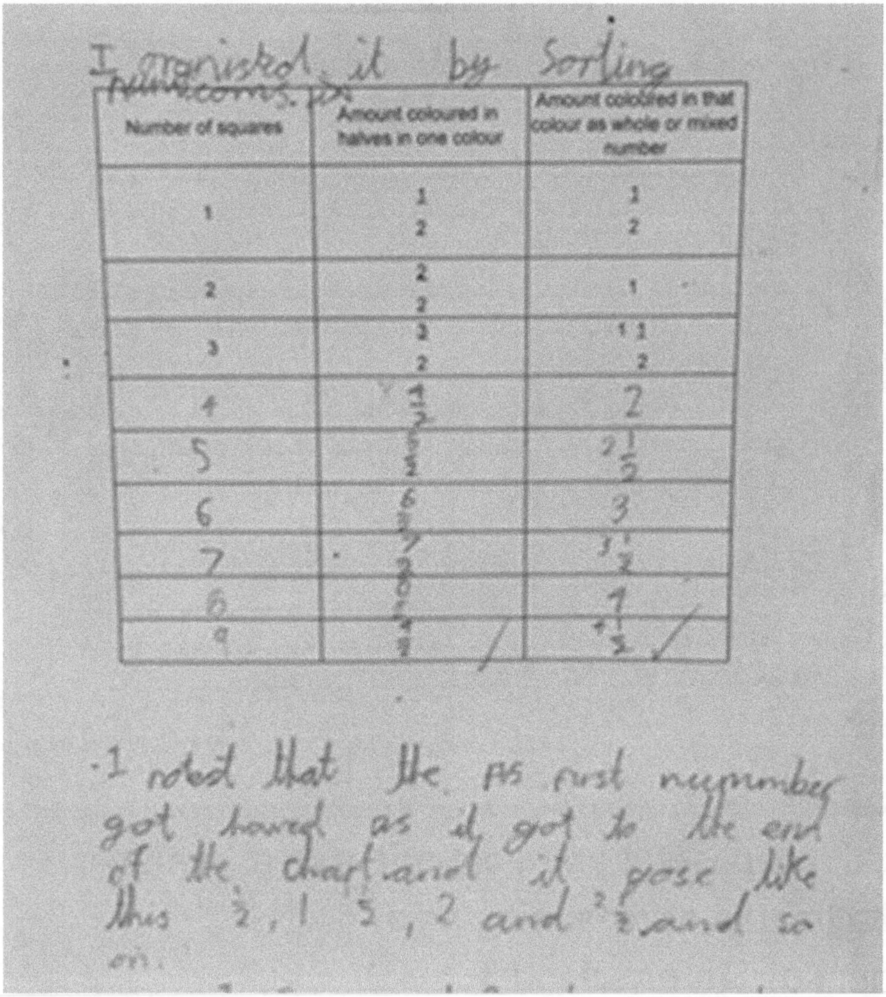

Figure 8.7 Learners record what they noticed

REFLECTION

How often should we plan opportunities for learners to reason?

You might even find that examples of reasoning begin to appear in other subjects. Figure 8.8 shows the beginning of a fairy tale that a 7-year-old was in the process of composing. The classic genre includes 'fairy tale land', the character 'Jack' (presumably from *Jack and the Beanstalk*) and a 'fairy Godmother', who was 'working systematically'!

Figure 8.8 A piece of writing that includes one of the skills of reasoning

Logical, purposeful and goal-orientated thinking: the hallmarks of reasoning as a mathematician or scientist

Throughout this book we have considered and explored some of the most pertinent and useful skills we believe to be essential for reasoning in primary mathematics and science. This chapter has reflected on what evidence of reasoning could look like. The section above offers some of the tangible ways in which we can collect this evidence; for example, through written, verbal or photographic evidence.

The following section reviews what many educators (e.g., Mason, 2009) consider to be among the most important hallmarks of reasoning. We have always maintained that all of the **skills of reasoning** are necessary and interdependent to each other. However, there are also steps that learners can take to improve, refine and develop their reasoning skills. In Chapter 1 we explored *how* we can potentially reason, by first noticing something, then by talking and listening to others, trying to make sense, sharing insights and then beginning the process of metacognition – the thinking about the thinking. At the outset, learners will begin to draw on skills such as describing, explaining, wondering, tinkering and questioning. For many this is where they may pause their reasoning. However, as teachers it is at this point that we might encourage them further to use other skills such as making predictions and conjectures, encouraging them to take their reasoning further to convince, justify, generalise and ultimately prove or disprove their thinking and reasoning.

If we want to gather evidence for reasoning, this is ultimately where we need to look.

Once learners have begun to make predictions, conjectures and hypotheses, the next step is for them to begin to justify these thoughts. Part of their justifications will be to offer generalisations, counter examples, notice if examples are typical or atypical and, finally, prove or disprove their thinking.

Predictions, conjectures and hypotheses

Chapter 5 explored the skills of prediction, conjecture and hypothesis in detail, so this section is a short summary to remind us of the importance of these skills.

In order to reason, learners need to be able to have something to think about and explore. Much of this thinking can come from establishing an atmosphere where predictions, conjectures and hypotheses are freely asked and valued. At this stage these assertions are simply statements, questions or rules that may be proved right or wrong.

It is also important to realise that doing mathematics and science involves making plenty of false predictions, conjectures or hypotheses. These are usually omitted from textbooks, perhaps because they make the pages look messy, or because it is thought a waste of time to follow a dead end? Perhaps there are many teachers and learners who perceive that the purpose of doing mathematics and science is to show what can be done, and not what cannot. However, asking a question, following a line of inquiry and testing it is at the heart of both mathematics and science, and is the start of learners' reasoning.

Generalising

A generalisation is a particularly important part of reasoning. To make a generalisation is to make an observation about something that is always true.

Examples in mathematics could include: diagonals of a square always bisect each other; why 4×9 is equal to 9×4. Generalisations in science include: the Sun always rises in the east; light reflects from a polished surface and the same angle as the angle of incidence; plants require some warmth to survive.

It is of course possible to make a generalisation about something that is not true or proved to be invalid. For example, if learners have only seen equilateral triangles, they are unlikely to be able to generalise the properties of all triangles, from just one specific example. This does not allow them to explore the underlying structure of triangles. However, such generalisations can be treated as conjectures or predictions which need to be explored and justified.

Generalising is about noticing patterns and properties that are common to many situations. It is about asking, *Will it always work?* A misconception is that a generalisation must be true. One way to test out generalisations is to specialise. For example, all odd numbers are one more than an even number. This is a generalisation. To prove it I need to find some examples or one counter example which would disprove it. I can start by specialising, with examples such as 3, 7, 9, 13, each of which can be viewed as an even number plus one more. However, while all generalisations do not have to emerge as a formula, particularly with primary-aged learners, it is useful to sometimes use the structure of number to justify whether the generalisation is true or not. In the example of odd numbers being one more than an even number, we can represent an odd number as $2n + 1$ (where n = positive integer). The +1 shows the property of odd numbers being one more than an even number, and the 2n shows the property of an even number as a number divisible by 2. Thus, $2n + 1$ is a generalisation for an odd number.

Generalisations, while particularly important within reasoning, are not limited to learners of a certain age. Very young learners continually make generalisations about the world in which they live. For example, they quickly realise that four-legged animals with a tail are called dogs. This is a generalisation. If they wanted to specialise they could suggest that ones with spots are also known as Dalmatians.

There are many educators (e.g., Johnston-Wilder and Mason, 2009) who believe that, *a lesson which fails to afford learners the opportunity to experience and express a generality cannot be considered to be a mathematics lesson.*

To be able to make generalisations learners need to draw on other **skills of reasoning**:

- predicting, conjecturing and hypothesising;

- offering counter examples;

- recognising prototypical and atypical examples;

- finding proof.

TRY THIS!

Deliberately give learners generalisations that are incorrect. For example, our plastic cylinder rolled furthest, so all cylinders will roll further than other 3D shapes.

Offering counter examples

We have mentioned counter examples elsewhere in the book. A counter example disproves a generalisation. These are best employed in context so we have another reason to explore some patently incorrect or contested predictions, conjectures or hypotheses. Thus learners get the chance to do what mathematicians and scientists do: disprove something and take the first step towards finding the truth.

Occasionally learners can offer a counter example to something that appears to disprove the generalisation, except that in a few cases it is actually a special case. For example, learners often form the generalisation that all prime numbers are odd. However, another learner may then point out that 2 is a prime number, which is also even. With this example, the generalisation requires some modification, so that learners may now say that all prime numbers above 2 are odd. This takes into account the special case.

Recognising prototypical and atypical examples

While being able to generalise is an important **skill of reasoning**, it is interesting to notice if learners are beginning to overgeneralise. This can be a consequence of using too many prototypical examples, where learners become used to a diet of the same type of examples. When this happens, they may begin to overgeneralise. For example, if learners have been taught to always subtract the smallest number from the biggest number, when they come across a calculation such as 34–56, they often change the calculation to 56–34, believing that perhaps the teacher or the textbook must be wrong. Other examples of overgeneralisations include multiplication makes bigger and all plants are green (because chlorophyll is green).

Try to use atypical examples within both mathematics and science. Not only will this help with learners' overgeneralising, but it will also enable opportunities for reasoning.

Finding proof

A proof is a logical deduction that can be found through different ways. We explored the different types of proof according to Pennant et al. (2014) in Chapter 2. Proof is a concept very important in mathematics and science, though in mathematics proof can mean proved forever, for example, $1 + 1 = 2$. In science, proof is conditional on no contradictory evidence being found; for example, for a time some considered the Piltdown Man (**www.nhm.ac.uk/ourscience/departments-and-staff/ library-and-archives/collections/piltdown-man.html**) to be plausible as the so-called 'missing link' between apes and humans. Fresh evidence revealed it to be a hoax.

In Chapter 2 we emphasised that all **skills of reasoning** are important and necessary. We do not view any of them as being more important than another. However, when evidencing reasoning if learners are justifying, generalising and seeking proof, they are using some of the most important hallmarks of being a mathematician or scientist, whatever their age.

CHAPTER SUMMARY

This chapter has sought to build on previous chapters and indicate the challenge to teachers of noticing and evidencing reasoning. This is important for teachers and for learners so that all are aware that reasoning is going on in classrooms and, with some consideration, can be developed further.

Having read this chapter you will:

- have a variety of ways to collect evidence of learners' reasoning;
- understand the different ways that learners can show how they are reasoning;
- know that one of the hallmarks of reasoning within mathematics and science is to be able to justify and prove or disprove your thinking.

9

A TOOLKIT OF IDEAS TO PROMOTE A CULTURE OF REASONING

IN THIS CHAPTER

By the end of this chapter you will:

- know how to develop a culture of reasoning across the school;
- have a toolkit of ideas to use with all stakeholders across the school;
- be inspired to promote reasoning across the school.

Introduction

Understanding is not something that anyone should tick off as 'completed'. Just when you think you understand, something else appears that offers another challenge. This is one of the reasons that the term 'mastery' often causes confusion and ambiguity. The term mastery suggests that if we have mastered something, this body of knowledge is complete. We would argue that a key element of true mastery is the recognition that one can still learn in this aspect of knowledge. Without this recognition we would risk becoming stale, perhaps even bored. One might ask about the great thinkers of history. Did they ever stop exploring their field? Enabling learners with the tools of reasoning is giving them permission to question, explain, hypothesise and justify. We want learners who are noticers, who are tinkerers, investigators, individuals who think about the world and about their own thinking. These learners are the inventors of the future!

This chapter serves as a toolkit for reasoning. It collects some of the 'Try This!' ideas from the previous eight chapters (as well as adding in different ones) and gathers them together in a way that allows you to begin to build a toolkit for reasoning, that in turn helps to promote a culture of reasoning across the school. At the end of the chapter we offer a 'reasoning rubric' and 'reasoning glossary' which you may find useful starting points in creating your own culture of reasoning.

All schools and learners are different and so it is reasonable to assume that you will need to choose which elements of this chapter are most applicable to your school situation. This desired culture of reasoning may represent a very significant shift. It might be from a place where what is to be learned is a fixed body of knowledge, to one where knowledge and understanding is expansive, where teachers and all children of any age are learners who seek challenge in thought and ideas.

What does a culture of reasoning look like?

The term 'culture' pre-supposes a way of life, where particular customs and beliefs are upheld and observed by a group at a particular time. Significantly, cultures can and do change.

Yet, current climates for both mathematics and science education may mean that reasoning has been overlooked or slimmed down recently. Pressures to get all learners to certain artificial expectations within a body of subject-specific content has dominated education policy in England (Alexander, 2010) and affected teaching practices. However, while classroom pedagogies may change, the need for learning does not. There are of course, certain elements of knowledge that need to be learned in both mathematics and science, but it is not just about memorising procedures and rules. Sometimes current policies can obscure the very essence of what mathematics and science is about: asking questions, taking risks, exploring processes, predicting, problem-solving, getting stuck, thinking and reasoning.

Perhaps the biggest change in culture may be around challenging the idea that mathematics and science are not solely about right or wrong answers. Many of our classrooms value this trait highly, and of course there is an aspect within both subjects that is concerned with obtaining particular answers to particular questions. But this is a small part of learning mathematics and science. Picture an iceberg. The top, visible part is about getting the right answers, but the larger unseen part is the understanding that leads to the answers. Within this part lies reasoning.

If adults and learners have been absorbed into the culture of getting the right answers, shifting to a culture that doesn't always value this in the same way may need some time and effort to develop.

As Sherman Stein (1996) was told by one student:

> *The teacher works one problem on the board and then we do twenty just like it.*
>
> *We don't have to know anything.*

Give teachers the quote from Sherman Stein and ask for their thoughts about it.

Who should be affected by a culture?

The word 'culture' implies social and other norms that are universal to those accepting it. To have a culture of reasoning in the school pre-supposes that all stakeholders in the school are knowledgeable and supportive about the culture upheld.

There are many people who are involved in school life and they all contribute to the culture of a school. However, some of these groups, or people within the groups may have a fixed vision of what the culture in the school is, or should, be. This could be for historical reasons, in that, We have always done things this way – a belief that the current culture works and so why change it, or a lack of understanding towards what the new culture can offer. Changing a culture takes time and that management of change needs support as well as challenge. The following section offers a selection of ideas which might be employed to shift perceptions.

Stakeholders in your school will include:

- learners;
- teachers;
- subject leaders/senior leaders;
- parents/carers;
- other employed adults;
- governors.

Some of the ideas below are included in the previous eight chapters, but others are new to this chapter. Here they are organised to support the different stakeholders.

Ideas to support learners to promote reasoning in their learning

- Engender a conjecturing or predicting atmosphere in the classroom, where all predictions and conjectures are valued and explored.
- Encourage competing conjectures and predictions, so that the idea of being right or wrong is not as important as justifying, explaining and proving.

- Ask learners to offer conjectures, predictions or hypotheses before embarking on an investigation or problem.

- Celebrate and value the state of being stuck.

- Encourage learners to use a variety of communication vehicles; e.g., drawing, role-play, verbal, written.

- Encourage variation in approaches.

- Remember that doing tasks is not learning, only an opportunity for learning, so build in 'reasoning time'.

- Provide plenty of examples where learners need to find a counter example and explain why.

- Encourage learners to notice patterns and discuss them.

- In mathematics or science lessons ask learners to pose five questions on a topic, which could be investigated. Then select the questions and coach learners to improve them.

- In lesson plenaries ask learners to reflect. What have I learned? How will this help me in the real world? Can I use this in other subjects? Do I now think differently?

- Ask learners to draw a picture of what it means to reason in mathematics or science.

- Introduce learners to some of the reasoning skills so they can begin to identify which ones they are using, and when.

- Deliberately give learners generalisations that are incorrect.

Ideas to support teachers to promote reasoning in their classrooms

- Ask teachers to draw a picture of what reasoning could look like in mathematics or science lessons.

- Visit an Early Years setting and look for evidence of reasoning in mathematics and science.

- Choose five or six reasoning skills, collate them onto a reasoning grid and stick it in the front of learners' books/folders. Ask them to indicate – both on the sheet and in their work – when they think they have been using one of the skills.

- Ask learners to use the reasoning skills to review their own reasoning.

- Try to include a 'reasoning' question every day.

- Build-in and teach the language of reasoning so that learners have the tools to participate.

- Create a reasoning working wall, where learners pose questions for other learners to begin pondering about.

- Insist that learners work together in pairs, trios and groups so they have opportunities to talk.

- Use a range of pedagogic constructs such as: same and different?; say what you see; another, and another; how many ways?; and doing and undoing.

- Ask Why? How? Could? Would? questions.

- In mathematics/science lessons ask learners if they can see the links between the two subjects.

- At the end of lessons ask learners to reflect on what they have learned, how this will help them in the real world, can the content and skills be transferred to other subjects and do they think differently about things now?

Ideas to support subject leaders/senior leaders to promote reasoning across the school

- Spend ten minutes in a staff meeting asking teachers to consider what the difference is between thinking and reasoning. Collate their responses on a flip chart and display in the staff room for a few weeks/half a term. Invite teachers and teaching staff to reflect on and add to the list.

- Go on a reasoning walk around the school. What evidence can you spot of learners' and adults' reasoning?

- Put into place a 'reasoning action plan' to span across the year. Introduce a different framework every term or half term.

- Consider setting up a reasoning club.

- Give teachers, or learners, a selection of the characteristics of reasoning and ask them to sort them, classify them and make connections between them.

- Ask teachers how they would draw a web of reasoning, using the reasoning skills.

- Collect together different question stems that teachers could use to promote reasoning.

- Invite a colleague from a different school to come and look for evidence of reasoning around the school.

- Play reasoning bingo. This game can be played with any of the stakeholders (e.g., learners, parents, governors). Give everyone a sheet with different skills of reasoning. Ask them to go and find evidence of these.

- Consider changing the mathematics marking policy so that reasoning is included within the mark scheme.

- Show teachers the importance of generality and how quickly and easily it can be incorporated into lessons.

- Visit an Early Years setting and look at the displays and materials. Can you see evidence of reasoning in mathematics and science?

- Visit an Early Years setting and talk to learners at play. Given a question, will they go a little deeper with Why? How? Could? Would?

- Why not survey your teachers/staff in school to discover their thoughts and views about reasoning?

- Find thought-provoking quotations involving reasoning and thinking for teaching staff to discuss and ponder over.

Ideas to support parents/carers to promote reasoning across the school

- Invite parents to a 'reasoning' workshop.

- Discuss how pages of calculations or copying out formulas are often the opposite to reasoning.

- Show how reasoning supports the skills of the future workforce.

Ideas to support other employed adults to promote reasoning across the school

- Ensure other adults have access to CPD for reasoning.

- Equip them with the reasoning sentence stems so they can either use them in their support work or encourage learners.

- Discuss the importance of using the correct mathematical or scientific language.

Ideas to support governors to promote reasoning across the school

- Invite governors into the school to observe learning but with their 'reasoning glasses' on.

- Ask a governor to take on the specific role as 'Reasoning Governor'.

- Offer training to governors on the difference between thinking and reasoning, and what they could be noticing when they are in the school.

- Ask governors if they are able to use their wider skills and invite people into school who use reasoning in their everyday lives.

Useful documents

This book has aimed to be a 'one stop shop' for teachers to improve, enhance and reflect on their approach to reasoning in primary mathematics and science classrooms. We have included some of the research surrounding thinking and reasoning, provided activities linked to mathematics and science that could enable reasoning, and also considered what the evidence of reasoning might look like. There are three more documents we feel would offer support: the reasoning survey that we referenced in Chapter 1, a reasoning rubric and a reasoning glossary.

A reasoning survey

Our definition of reasoning and its associated skills has of course been influenced by many factors: the conversations we have had with teachers and other educators; the literature we have read; the elements we consider important within mathematical and scientific proficiency. However, we have tried to offer a broad and balanced view. One of the early activities we used was a survey that we asked teachers to complete. This gave us a baseline from which to begin framing our views of reasoning.

We have included the reasoning survey here and suggest it could be a starting point for schools to begin conversations about developing a culture of reasoning.

Please tell us about your understanding of reasoning in primary education.

Which one of the following requires reasoning?

- You think about which night you will meet a friend.   Y or N

- You consider the pros and cons of a holiday destination.   Y or N

- You question a friend about why they voted one way in a referendum?   Y or N

- You reflect on an event and why it was successful.   Y or N

At what age to people begin to reason? 1–3 yrs, 4–6 yrs, 7–11 yrs, 11–15 yrs

In which subjects can learners reason? English, maths, science, art, history, geography, music, RE, PE, ML (then underline the strongest three for reasoning).

What features of a classroom would make it conducive to reasoning? Open-ended questioning, child-led discussions, child-led activity, closed questions, encouragement, acceptance of non-conventional responses, overly teacher-directed activity, exploratory activity.

Would you say that reasoning is an innate skill or one that can be learned? innate / learned

In order that children can learn this subject they need to reason:	Tick to indicate not at all	a little	somewhat	a great deal
mathematics				
science				
English				
DT				
art and design				
music				
history				
geography				
RE				
PE				
ML				

In your role as a professional teacher how important is it that you reason?

not at all / somewhat / a great deal

Is reasoning straightforward to teach?   Yes / No

Please add any other comments or thoughts about reasoning in the primary classroom and in particular in relation to mathematics and science.

A reasoning rubric

The reasoning rubric is a collection of possible aspects you might be looking for in and around school. It could be used by individual teachers, subject leaders or senior leaders (including governors) and learners to observe and notice if reasoning is present across the school. It is not meant to be a checklist, nor would we expect all aspects to be present all the time. It is offered as a guide; a starting point.

Aspect of reasoning	Possible evidence (e.g.)
Learners are grappling with understanding, rather than just memorising or applying rules automatically.	Learners' books/whiteboards show different ways of solving problems, rather than just one way.
There are lots of questions being asked (by learners and adults).	Both teachers and learners are asking questions of each other and their peers.
Learners are discussing and answering questions in sentences, using words such as, because, I think, the reasons for...	Can you make a parallelogram whose opposite angles are not equal? I cannot make a parallelogram whose opposite angles are not equal because a parallelogram has two pairs of parallel sides, meaning the opposite angles will be equal.
Learners are active in their learning (as opposed to learning passively).	Learners are constructing their knowledge through using equipment, testing equipment, etc. The teacher is acting as an activator, not facilitator.
The idea of being right or wrong is not as important as the process involved.	Examples on the board include incorrect solutions. Learners learn about scientists who experienced failure prior to success; for example, Edison's development of the light bulb.
Learners are being asked to predict, offer conjectures and make hypotheses.	On the classroom wall learners record their predictions to events.
Teachers are using questions such as, What is the same or different?, What do you notice?, and Give me another, and another.	Work in learners' books shows problems and investigations initiated by such questions.
Learners plan and solve problems and investigations.	Less work in books but learners are spending longer thinking and reasoning.
Marking refers to aspects of reasoning.	Convince me there are no other solutions. Do these results confirm your hypothesis?
There is evidence of a reasoning culture around the school.	Lesson objectives include both subject-specific content and skills of reasoning; vocabulary on display includes the skills of reasoning; exhibits of learners' work show different methods to the same problem.
Learners are very positive about their learning in mathematics and science.	I am good at maths because I convinced my partner; I love science lessons because we get to plan experiments.
There is evidence of typical and atypical examples.	2D shapes are presented in different orientations.
Learners generate lots of answers to the same concept so they can begin to spot patterns.	Learners considering deforestation are challenged to suggest five potential solutions and then consider an overall plan.

(Continued)

(Continued)

Aspect of reasoning	Possible evidence (e.g.)
Teachers are employing a reasoning scaffold (e.g., NRICH, BLOOM) to consider the progression for reasoning.	I can see you have explained your approach, but can you now convince me it is correct?
Teachers provide impossible questions that cannot be answered with a correct solution.	Can you find a multiple of 6 that is not a multiple of 3?
Teachers give control to the learners.	Options for investigation of shape/materials are selected by groups in the class.
Learners apply learning to real-life examples.	Learners measure the height of trees in the local park.
Learners apply their reasoning skills outside the classroom.	The school council suggests a series of actions to help understand the problem of children littering.
Sets of questions are collected.	At the start of a topic, learners pose questions about things that had puzzled them.

A reasoning glossary

The definitions we have provided, along with the examples, are our interpretations of these words and phrases, which we have viewed though a reasoning lens. We are not offering them up as *the* definitive definitions; indeed you may have your own interpretations of these words and phrases, which are equally valid.

Word/phrase	Definition	Mathematics example	Science example
Working abstractly	Where rules and concepts are derived from specific, real-life examples.	If I have three oranges and two apples I have a total of five pieces of fruit. $3 + 2 = 5$.	Big objects are observed to roll further so we test a hypothesis: all large balls roll furthest.
Agreeing/ disagreeing	To be/not to be of the same mind or opinion.	I agree that sometimes adding one more to a number makes it bigger, but disagree this is not a general rule.	I know that metals can be magnetic, but are all metals magnetic?
Altering	When we alter the question to make the understanding easier but the original question/ concept remains.	Exploring the constant difference in subtraction. $123 - 19$ has the same difference as $124 - 20$ but perhaps the second calculation is easier?	Our initial question was, Which material is the best? We realised that we had to explain the word best.

Classifying	Organise into groups based on observable criteria.	We classified the shapes according to their number of sides.	We classified the 15 different leaves based on their shape and texture.
Comparing	To note the similarity or dissimilarity between objects or ideas.	What is the same and different between one and 1?	A toad is similar to a frog but the skin is usually dull coloured and warty looking.
Conjecturing	Offering a thought or idea.	I conjecture that the sum of three consecutive numbers is divisible by 3.	I conjecture that sounds only travel in a straight line.
Convincing	To persuade and make someone certain.	If I am convinced that 3 is more than 2, and 4 is more than 3, then 4 is more than 2.	After several different tests I am convinced that greater air resistance slows objects down.
Correcting	To rectify or put right.	Correct the calculation $100 + 1 = 1001$.	We realised that at the start the temperature of each cup of water should be the same.
Decomposing	Taking an idea apart.	I can decompose 21 into $19 + 2$; $15 + 6$; $11 + 10$.	We can examine each step in a food chain to describe the relationship between one living thing and another.
Deconstructing	To take apart or examine something.	With the calculation $178 - 36$ I can either solve this by finding the difference, by altering the calculation or by taking away.	We can follow the path of light reflecting off different mirrors to find its source.
Deleting	To consider what can be deleted without affecting the problem.	Hedgehog flavoured crisps cost 75p per packet. How much would six packets cost? I can delete the flavour of the crisps without altering the problem itself.	To predict the apparent shape of the Moon tomorrow night we consult our notes from the last 30 nights.
Describing	To provide an account of something.	An equilateral triangle is a triangle where all the sides and angles are equal.	When we increased the pull on the elastic it pushed the car further.
Doing/undoing	Most actions have a corresponding action, so with any doing there is an associated undoing.	Solve the calculation $12 + 12$; or the answer is 24, what is the question?	After completing a circuit it was taken apart and reconnected to add more bulbs.

(Continued)

(Continued)

Word/phrase	Definition	Mathematics example	Science example
Exemplifying	To exemplify or clarify with an example.	Multiplying does not always make a number bigger. For example, $\frac{1}{2} \times 2 = 1$.	There is a clear fossil record showing the evolution of the horse.
Explaining	To make clear an idea or situation.	A prime number is a number that has only 1 and itself as factors.	The planets all orbit the Sun in the same direction. This indicates that they formed from a rotating disc on material.
Extrapolating	To estimate or predict beyond the values given.	If I eat one chocolate on day 1 and then two chocolates on day 2, and keep doubling the quantity each day, on day 5 I will have 16 chocolates to eat.	Looking at our graph of average heights for children in our school we can say that a 12-year-old will be around 155 cm tall.
Evaluating	To judge or determine the importance or value of something.	With the question on bus timetables do I need to use the picture of the bus in order to work out when the bus departs and arrives?	We asked whether red squirrels should be protected at any cost.
Generalising	Applying a rule to other examples and aspects in the world.	The sum of any two odd numbers is always even.	We know that light travels in straight lines, which explains how shadows have a shape and why we can't see around corners.
Hypothesising	A rule that we might hope to establish as a generalisation, law or theorem.	Multiplication always makes numbers bigger.	Yellow objects always float.
Interpolating	To construct new data within given points.	If 100% = £60 then I know that 75% = £45.	After six minutes the temperature was 20°C, after 12 minutes it was 30°C, what was the reading at 9 minutes.
Making judgements	To reach a decision or conclusion.	I conclude the shape to be a cube, based on the fact that it is a regular hexahedron and all its faces are square.	Our investigation of materials showed that our prediction was incorrect as the best thermal insulator we tested was bubble plastic.

Justifying	To provide sensible reasons.	Multiplying by 10 is not the same as adding a zero to the number; e.g., $3.4 \times 10 = 34$ not 3.40.	We will repeat the test ten times so that we can be confident in a mean value.
Being logical	A particular way of thinking that uses rules to reason within that particular system.	$3x + 2 = 14$. $3 \times 4 = 12$. $12 + 2 = 14$. $x = 4$.	Sound gets fainter as it travels because it spreads out and energy is lost as it bumps into molecules in the air.
Making connections	Observing connections between ideas, events, facts, rather than separate and disjointed.	$3 + 3 + 3 + 3$ is equivalent to 3×4.	Energy is all around us in different forms, e.g., light, sound, electricity, movement.
Noticing	To pay attention to or to observe something.	If I am given the calculation $161 \div 7 = 23$, I notice that $168 \div 7$ is 7 more so the answer is 24.	We noticed that the temperature rose at a constant rate.
Observing	To perceive something using your senses.	This line is parallel and this one is perpendicular.	Features of one plant are similar to, but not identical to, those on another plant species observed.
Offering counter examples	To demonstrate that a generalisation is not valid.	2 is a prime number and so disproves that all prime numbers are odd.	After generalising that all plants are green, research reveals plants like Copper Beech with purple foliage, which disproves the generalisation.
Organising	To arrange, sort and put things in order.	Order numbers according to how many factors they have.	Order graphs according to how steep they are on a given interval.
Pattern seeking	To identify either something that can be copied or arranged in an order to a rule.	1, 3, 6, 10, 15 is the pattern of triangular numbers.	The shadow cast by the shadow stick followed the same pattern each day we had sunshine.
Playing	To engage in an activity for enjoyment.	Trying to find the biggest number.	Making a parachute for a toy animal.
Predicting	To offer an estimate or a consequence of a future event.	I can predict that 1,004 is divisible by 4 because I know the rules of dividing by 4.	I predicted that all these materials would conduct electricity.

(Continued)

(Continued)

Word/phrase	Definition	Mathematics example	Science example
Proving	To demonstrate beyond doubt.	I can prove that the angles of a triangle add up to 180° using paper and scissors.	I can prove that dragging the box over some materials requires a greater force.
Puzzling	To come across something that is difficult to understand or explain at first.	I am puzzled how adding a negative number to another negative number results in a smaller number. I thought that addition made answers bigger in value.	We puzzled over a NASA picture of an eclipse of the Sun by Saturn. Where was the camera positioned?
Questioning	To elicit information or confirm understanding.	What is it about this object that makes it a cuboid?	What affects the speed at which the parachute falls? Is it the mass or the string length?
Recognising links	To be able to use what you know to work out something you don't know.	Between any two decimals there is another decimal.	The Moon appeared to be this shape two nights ago and this shape tonight, tomorrow it will be …
Refuting	To prove that something is incorrect.	In a triangle two angles are equal but all three edges are different in length.	Turning the seed over does not make the root grow up. Our observation of different seeds shows this.
Sorting	Grouping together things with common attributes.	These 3D shapes have eight vertices or fewer.	This is a group of oval leaves.
Specialising	Constructing particular examples to see what happens.	$7 \times 8 = 56$, so I have specialised to generalise that an odd number multiplied by an even number results in an even number.	We tested five materials to see which was strongest. We now see that man-made material is very strong.
Speculating	To have a theory or conjecture about something without firm evidence.	The denominator of a fraction is always bigger than the numerator.	Our seedling will not germinate in sand.
Being systematic	To employ a methodical system.	To work out all the possibilities for the different combinations I can make with three 1p, 2p and 5p coins, I am going to start with all the variations with 1p coins.	I designed a fair test to see which material would be best for sunglasses.

Tinkering	To make small changes to something.	Change 0.333 so that it is equivalent to $\frac{1}{3}$.	We tried four different switches in our circuit. The push switch worked best.
Verifying	To confirm or prove that something is true or not.	What additional properties must be added so that a rectangle is also a square?	We increased the voltage which made our electromagnet stronger. Decreasing the voltage made the electromagnet weaker.
Visualising	To form a picture of something in your head.	Can you visualise what a parallelogram looks like?	Can you visualise the habitat of an arctic fox?
Wondering	To be curious, to want to know something.	I wonder what would happen if I cut a piece of the square from one side and attached it to another. I wonder what shape it would now make?	One child wondered, where does the Sun go at night?
Working backwards	To start at the end and work backwards to get to the beginning.	I have arrived at school. Which directions did I take to get here?	The (safe) mixture is fizzing, what ingredients were mixed to cause this?

CHAPTER SUMMARY

This chapter is the culmination of numerous ideas in this book, but gathered together in a different way to enable you to begin to consider building a culture of reasoning across the school. It has considered the different stakeholders involved and offered suggestions as to how to involve them all, which is necessary if you want a whole-school shift in culture. This chapter, along with the previous eight, has given you the tools to start you on your reasoning journey.

Having read this chapter you will:

- have considered how to begin to create a culture of reasoning across the school;
- have a toolkit of ideas to use with all stakeholders across the school;
- be inspired to enable reasoning across the school.

10
FINAL REMARKS

This book was born from a desire to guide primary teachers and to encourage them to reason about reasoning in the classroom. Learners benefit from reflective, thoughtful teachers who constantly revisit and revise pedagogical approaches. A focus on learner reasoning gives, we feel, a powerful direction to this self-reflective approach. Consider:

- is there part of your mathematics and science teaching which could further promote reasoning?

- how would learners respond to more opportunity to reason?

- how could you activate rather than facilitate reasoning?

- are there colleagues who might join you in this journey?

- from our 45 skills of reasoning which will you now promote and develop?

- are you now reasoning about reasoning in the classroom?

We have said that reasoning is the currency of the future for learners but it is more than this for teachers; it represents a shift of perspective away from more traditional approaches of pupil learning towards one where learners are meaning makers.

You will find that this book is a resource for teachers and teacher educators. It provides a toolkit of ideas and explores many of the hallmarks of reasoning. The book identifies key areas of reasoning in primary mathematics and science by:

- offering a wealth of opportunities to **reason about reasoning** through the Reflection, Reasoning Focus and Try This! boxes;

- exploring the difference between thinking and reasoning;

- exemplifying different frameworks to underpin reasoning in the classroom;

- bringing together 45 reasoning skills, with a reasoning glossary and subject-specific examples;

- exemplifying four key **skills of reasoning**, dedicating a chapter to each one;

- providing 70+ classroom activities in mathematics and science;

- offering a rubric for reasoning;

- including a reasoning survey to try out with different stakeholders across the school;

- making reference to some of the pertinent literature around reasoning in mathematics and science;

- exploring how to evidence reasoning;

- considering how to create and build a culture of reasoning.

APPENDIX

Chapter 1

Reasoning 1 possible solutions

$14 \times 5 = ?$

$14 \times 5 = (10 \times 5) + (4 \times 5)$

$14 \times 5 = 14 + 14 + 14 + 14 + 14$

$14 \times 5 = (7 \times 5) + (7 \times 5)$

$(14 \times 10)/2$

$15 \times 5 - (1 \times 5)$

$5 \times 14 = 5 + 5 + 5 + 5 + 5 + 5 + 5 + 5 + 5 + 5 + 5 + 5 + 5 + 5$

Reasoning 2 solution

Yes, because the Moon spins once every 28 Earth days. So all parts of the lunar surface have around 14 Earth days of dark followed by 14 Earth days of light. Could you explain this to another person?

Chapter 4

Toolkit of questions

Questions to compare, sort and organise, to probe the evidence

What is the same and what is different?

Can you sort these by ...?

Can you organise these by ...?

How many ...?

What is ...?

Which is the odd one out?

Why have you sorted in this way?

Why do you think that ...?

Do you have evidence of ...?

Questions to change or alter, to question the question

What if ...?

What happens if we change ...?

If this is the answer, what is the question?

Why don't you try ...?

Have you thought about ...?

Do you have a question about ...?

Could you alter ...?

Could you try ...?

Is there a quicker way?

What kind of question is this?

Is there an easier way?

Why might you change ...?

Are we any closer to answering the question?

Questions to conjecture, hypothesise and generalise, to test implications and consequences

Can you give an example?

Do you agree?

What do you think might happen?

Can you offer a conjecture/hypothesis?

What happens in general?

Is there a general rule for that?

Can you spot a pattern?

From your ideas, can we work out ...?

Is it always, sometimes or never true?

Is this a special example?

Has this happened before?

What do you notice?

How could you test to see if ...?

Why is this a generalisation?

What happens if ...?

What do you think is going on?

Why do you think that ...?

Can you give me a counter example?

Questions to explain, justify and convince, to seek clarification

Can you explain why ...?

Can you explain your thinking?

Can you give a reason why ...?

How would you explain?

How does that help?

How would you justify?

What do you mean by ...?

How would you convince?

Who would you like to convince?

What helped you to ...?

Can you give me another example?

Is there another ...?

Can you find an example that doesn't ...?

When would you use this approach?

Does anyone have a question to ask?

Questions to support either the completion, alteration or deletion of work

What needs to be changed so that ...?

What can be added to ...?

What can be removed so that ...?

What needs to change?

Is there a different point of view?

Have you considered ...?

If I do ... what will the effect be?

List of questions compiled and adapted from various sources including Grigg (2015), Jeffcoat et al. (2004) and Watson and Mason (1998).

BIBLIOGRAPHY

ACME (2016) *Problem Solving in Mathematics: Realising the Vision Through Better Assessment*. London: The Royal Society.

Ahlberg, J and Ahlberg, A (1999) *Funnybones*. London: Penguin Books.

Alexander, R (2008) *Towards Dialogic Teaching*. Cambridge: Dialogos.

Alexander, R (ed) (2010) *Children, Their World, Their Education*. London: Routledge.

Alexander, R J (2017a) *Towards Dialogic Teaching: Rethinking Classroom Talk* (5th edition). Cambridge: Dialogos.

Alexander, R J (2017b) Developing Dialogue: Process, Trial, Outcomes (full account of research) Accessed March 2018 at: **www.robinalexander.org.uk/dialogic-teaching**

Anderson, L W and Krathwohl, D R (eds) (2001) *A Taxonomy for Learning, Teaching, and Assessing: A Revision of Bloom's Taxonomy of Educational Objectives*. Boston: Allyn & Bacon (Pearson Education Group).

Askew, M (2012) *Transforming Primary Mathematics*. London: Routledge.

Barmby, P, Bilsborough, L, Harries, T and Higgins, S (2009) *Primary Mathematics, Teaching for Understanding*. Berkshire: Open University Press/McGraw Hill.

Barnes, D (1992) *From Communication to Curriculum* (2nd edition). London: Heinemann.

Barton, D (2008) Early Years Science Is So Much More Than Just Knowledge and Understanding of the World. *Primary Science 111* Jan/Feb 2010 5–7, Hatfield: ASE.

Blanton, M, Stephens, A, Knuth, E, Gardiner, A M, Isler, I, and Kim, J S (2015) The development of children's algebraic thinking: the impact of a comprehensive early algebra intervention in third grade. *Journal for Research in Mathematics Education*, 46: 39–87.

Bloom, B S (ed), Engelhart, M D, Furst, E J, Hill, W H and Krathwohl, D R (1956) *Taxonomy of Educational Objectives. Handbook I: The Cognitive Domain*. New York: David McKay Co Inc.

Bloom, B S (1968) Learning for Mastery. Instruction and Curriculum. Regional Education Laboratory for the Carolinas and Virginia, *Topical Papers and Reprints, Number 1*. Evaluation comment, 1, n2.

Bloom, B S (1971a) Individual Differences in School Achievement – A Vanishing Point: A Monograph. Aera-pdk Award Lecture Annual Meeting American Educational. *Research Association*. New York February 6, 1971, Phi Delta Kappa.

Bloom, B S (1971b) Mastery Learning. In Block, J H (ed) *Mastery Learning Theory and Practice*. New York: Holt, Rinehart & Winston.

Boaler, J (2016) *Mathematical Mindsets*. San Francisco: Jossey-Bass.

Borthwick, A (2008) *Children's Perceptions of, and Attitudes Towards Mathematics Lessons in Primary Schools*. Unpublished Thesis: University of East Anglia.

Brown, E (2009) *Handa's Surprise*. London: Walker Books.

Bruner, J S (1966) *Toward a Theory of Instruction*. Cambridge: Harvard University Press.

Computing at School (CAS) (2013) *Computing in the National Curriculum: A Guide for Primary Teachers*. London: NACCCE.

Cross, A and Board, J (2014) *Creative Ways to Teach Primary Science*. London: OUP.

Cross, A and Board, J (2015) Playground Science. *Primary Science 136* Jan/Feb. 2015 24–26, Hatfield: ASE.

Cross, A and Borthwick, A (2016) *Connecting Primary Maths and Science*. London: Open University Press/McGraw Hill.

Cross, A and Borthwick, A (2017) Reasoning in Primary Mathematics and Science. Proceedings of the 18th International Conference of Teaching, Education and Learning, Bangkok, 19–20 July.

Cross, A, Borthwick, A, Beswick, K, Board, J and Chippendall, J (2016) *Curious Learners in Primary Maths, Science, Computing and DT*. London: Sage.

Crossland, J (2015) Thinking About Metacognition. *Primary Science 138* May/June 2015 14–16 Hatfield: ASE.

Crossland, J (2017) Optimal learning in schools – theoretical evidence: Part 4 Metacognition. *School Science Review, June*, 98(365): 47–55

Darwin, C (1859) *On the Origin of the Species by Means of Natural Selection*. London: John Murray.

De Boo, M (2006) Science in the Early Years, in Harlen, W (ed) *ASE Guide to Primary Science Education*. Hatfield: ASE.

Deighton, K, Morrice, M and Overton, D (2011) Vocabulary in four to eight-year-old children in inner city schools. *Journal of Emergent Science*, March 2017, 13: 7–13. Hatfield: Emergent Science Network/ASE.

Department for Children, Schools and Families/Qualifications and Curriculum Development Agency (2010) *The National Curriculum Primary Handbook*. London: DCSF/QCDA.

Devlin, K (1991) *Logic and Information*. Cambridge: Cambridge University Press.

DfE (1995a) *Mathematics in the National Curriculum*. London, HMSO.

DfE (1995b) *Science in the National Curriculum*. London: Crown Copyright.

DfE (2012) *Development Matters*. London: HMSO. Accessed January 2018 at: **www.foundation years.org.uk/wp-content/uploads/2012/03/Development-Matters-FINAL-PRINT-AMENDED.pdf**

DfE (2014) *The National Curriculum in England: Key Stages 1 and 2*. London: HMSO.

Dillon, J T (1985) Using questions to foil discussion. *Teaching and Teacher Education*, 1(2): 109–121.

Dillon, J T (1994) *Using Discussion in Classrooms*. Buckingham: Open University Press.

Dorling Kindersley (2010) *Space: A Children's Encylopedia*. London: Dorling Kindersley.

Dossey, J (2017) Problem Solving from a Mathematical Viewpoint. In Csapo, B and Funke, J (eds) *The Nature of Problem Solving: Using Research to Inspire 21st Century Learning*. Paris: OECD Publishing. (Available at **http://dx.doi.org/10.1787/9789264273955-en**)

Dweck, C S (1986) Motivational processes affecting learning. *American Psychologist*, 41: 1040. Washington: American Psychologist Association.

Gatt, S and Theuma, G (2012) Inquiry-based learning in the early years through story telling. *Journal of Emergent Science*, 4, Winter 2012: 19–24. Hatfield: ESN/ASE.

Gifford, S (2017) *Developing Pattern Awareness with Young Children*. Cambridge: NRICH. Accessed January 2018 at: **www.nrich.maths.org/10990**

Gleick, J (1988) *Chaos: Making a New Science*. London: Heineman.

Godec, S, King, H, and Archer, L (2017) *The Science Capital Teaching Approach: Engaging Students with Science Promoting Social Justice*. London: University College London. Accessed March 2018 at: **www.ucl.ac.uk/ioe/departments-centres/departments/education-practice-and-society/science-capital-research/science-capital-teaching-approach-pack**

Goldsworthy, A and Feasey, R (1997) *Making Sense of Primary Science Investigations*. Hatfield: ASE.

Grigg, R (2015) *Becoming an Outstanding Teacher*. London: Routledge.

Fay, T H and Greef, J C (2006) Lion, wildebeest and zebra: a predator-prey model. *Ecological Modelling No.196: 237–244*. Elsevier. Available at: **http://people.kzoo.edu/barth/math280/articles/lion_wildebeest_zebra.pdf**

Fisher, R (1998) *Teaching Thinking: Philosophical Enquiry in the Classroom*. London: Continuum.

Fisher, R (2005) *Teaching Children to Think*. Cheltenham: Stanley Thornes.

Flavell, J (1979) Metacognition and cognitive monitoring: a new area of cognitive-development inquiry. *American Psychologist*, 34(10): 906–911.

Fowler and Fowler (1984) *The Pocket Oxford Dictionary*. Oxford: Clarendon Press.

Fromental, J L (2006) *365 Penguins*. New York: Abrams.

Johnston, J (2009) Exploratory play and emergence in a conversational approach. *Emergent Science Newsletter*, 4(5): 16–20. Hatfield: ESN/ASE.

Johnston-Wilder, S and Mason, J (2009) *Developing Thinking in Geometry*. London: Sage Publications Ltd.

Hattie, J (2009) *Visible Learning: A Synthesis of Over 800 Meta-Analyses Relating to Achievement*. Abingdon: Routledge. Harvard University. Visible Thinking. Accessed January 2018 at: **www.pz.harvard.edu/projects/visible-thinking**

Haylock, D (2006) *Maths Explained for Primary Teachers*. London: Sage.

Haylock, D (2010) *Mathematics Explained for Primary Teachers*. London: Sage.

Howe, A, Collier, C, McMahon, K, Earle, S and Davies, D (2017) *Science 5–11 A Guide for Teachers* (3rd edition). London: David Fulton.

Hughes, C (2012) *Little Kids First Big Book of Space*. Washington: National Geographic.

Inhelder, B and Piaget, J (1958) *The Growth of Logical Thinking from Childhood to Adolescence*. New York: Basic Books.

Jeffcoat, M, Jones, M, Mansergh, J, Mason, J, Sewell, H and Watson, A (2004) *Primary Questions and Prompts*. Derby: Association of Teachers of Mathematics.

Jones, R J (2012) *Look Inside Space*. London: Usborne Publishing.

Kallery, M (2000) Making the most of questions and ideas in the early years. *Primary Science Review* 61, Jan/Feb: 18–19. Hatfield: ASE.

Kaput, J (1992) Technology and Mathematics Education, in D A Grouws (ed), *Handbook of Research on Mathematics Teaching and Learning*. New York: NCTM.

Kilpatrick, J, Swafford, J and Findell, B (2001) *Adding it Up: Helping Children Learn Mathematics*. Washington: National Academies Press.

Langer, E J (1997) *The Power of Mindful Learning*. Cambridge: Da Capo Press.

Luckin, R, Baines, E, Cukurova, M and Holmes, W (2017) *Solved! Making the Case for Collaborative Problem-Solving*. London: NESTA

Martin, M O, Mulis, I V S, Foy, P and Hooper, M (2016) TIMSS 2015 International Results in Science. Boston College: International Association for the Evaluation of Educational Achievement. (Summaries available at: **http://timssandpirls.bc.edu/timss2015/international-results/timss-2015/science/student-achievement/**)

Mason, J (1999) *Learning and Doing Mathematics* (2nd revised edition). St. Albans: Tarquin.

Mason, J, Burton L and Stacey, B (2010) *Thinking Mathematically*. Essex: Pearson.

Mercer, N (2008) Classroom dialogue and the teacher's role. *Education Review*, 21(1): 60–65.

Mercer, N and Littlejohn, K (2007) *Dialogue and the Development of Children's Thinking: A Sociocultural Approach*. London: Routledge.

Mercer, N, Dawes, L, Wegerif, R and Sams, C (2004) Reasoning as a scientist: ways of helping children to use language to learn science. *British Educational Research Journal*, 30(3): 367–385.

Mercer, N, Dawes, L and Staarman, J (2009) Dialogic teaching in the primary science classroom. *Language and Education*, 23(4): 353–363.

Milbourne, A and Riglietti, S (2008) *How Big is a Million?* London: Scholastic.

Mulis, Martin, Foy and Hooper (2016) TIMSS 2015 International Results in Mathematics. Boston College: International Association for the Evaluation of Educational Achievement. Available at: **http://timss2015.org/#/?playlistId=0&videoId=0**

National Council of Teachers of Mathematics (NCTM) (1989) *Curriculum and Evaluation Standards for School Mathematics*. Reston: NCTM.

Naylor, S and Keogh, B (2010) *Concept Cartoons*. Northwich: Millgate House.

Nunes, T, Bryant, P, Sylva, K and Barros, R (2009) *Development of Maths Capabilities and Confidence in Primary School*. London: DCSF.

Organisation for Economic Co-operation and Development (OECD) (2015) *Draft Collaborative Problem-Solving Framework*. Paris: OECD.

Organisation for Economic Co-operation and Development (OECD) (2017) *Results in Focus*. Paris: OECD.

Papic, M, Mulligan, J and Mitchelmore, M (2011) Assessing the development of pre-schoolers' mathematical patterning. *Journal for Research in Mathematics Education*, 42(3): 237–268.

Pennant, J, Woodham, L and Bagnall, B (2014) Reasoning: the journey from novice to expert. Cambridge: NRICH. Accessed January 2018 at: **www.nrich.maths.org/10990**

Piaget, J (1958) *The Child's Construction of Reality*. London: Routledge and Kegan Paul.

Piaget, J (1970) *Genetic Epistemology*. New York: Columbia University Press.

Polya, G (1945) *How to Solve It*. Princeton: Princeton University Press.

Reznitskaya, A (2012) Rethinking language use during literature discussions. *The Reading Teacher*, 65(7): 446–456.

Rittle-Johnson, B, Fyfe, E R, Hofer, K G and Farran, D C (2016) Early math trajectories: low income children's trajectory mathematics knowledge from ages 4 to 11. *Child Development*, 88(5): 1727–1742. doi:10.1111/cdev.12662

Ryan, J and Williams, J (2007) *Children's Mathematics 4–15*. Berkshire: Open University Press/McGraw-Hill Education.

Sayre, A P (2006) *One is a Snail, Ten is a Crab*. London: Walker Books.

Sharratt, N (2010) *Foggy Foggy Forest*. London: Walker Books.

Standards and Testing Agency (STA) (2016a) *2016 National Curriculum Tests: Key Stage 2*. London: STA.

Standards and Testing Agency (STA) (2016b) *2016 Teacher Assessment Exemplification: End of Key Stage 2 Science*. London: STA.

Standards and Testing Agency (STA) (2017) *2014 Science Sampling Tests: Commentary and Selected Questions*. London: Standards and Testing Agency.

Stein, S (1996) Gresham's Law: algorithm drives out thought. *Humanistic Mathematics Network*, 13: 25.

Swan, M (2006) Designing and using research instruments to describe the beliefs and practices of mathematics teachers. *Research in Education*, 75: 58–70.

Tapson, F (1996) *The Oxford Mathematics Study Dictionary*. Oxford: Oxford University Press.

The Royal Society (1985) *The Public Understanding of Science*. London: The Royal Society.

The Royal Society (2014) *Vision for Science and Mathematics Education*. London: The Royal Society.

Turner, J, Keogh, B, Naylor, S and Lawrence, L (2011) *It's Not fair, or Is It?* Sandbach: Millgate House.

Turner, S (2012) It's Not Fair! *Primary Science No.121 Jan/Feb*: 30–33. Hatfield: ASE.

Vanstone, E (2016) Cornflour gloop and fizzy potions … making counting count! *Primary Science 145 Nov/Dec*. Hatfield: ASE.

Vygotsky, L S (1962) *Thought and Language*. Cambridge: Massachusetts Institute of Technology.

Vygotsky, L S (1978) Interaction Between Learning and Development, in Gauvain and Cole (eds) *Readings on the Development of Children*. New York: Scientific American Books, 34–40.

Watson, A and Mason, J (1998) *Questions and Prompts for Mathematical Thinking*. Derby: ATM.

Welcome Trust (2017) *'State of the Nation' Report of UK Primary Science Education*. London: CFE/Welcome.

White, M (2007) *Galileo Antichrist: A Biography*. London: Weidenfeld and Nicolson.

Williams, F (1969) Models for encouraging creativity in the classroom by integrating cognitive-affective behaviours. *Educational Technology*, 9(12): 7–13.

Woodham, L (2014) *Using NRICH Tasks to Develop Key Problem-Solving Skills*. Accessed January 2018 at: **https://nrich.maths.org/11082**

INDEX

Note: Page numbers in **bold** refer to the reasoning glossary.